WE BEHELD HIS GLORY

(A study of God's revelation of himself to the World)

RONNIE BURKE

Dedication

Special thanks to my friend Michael Rodriguez, who was my reader
and critic of the book

About The Author

Dr Ronnie Burke is a native of Lake Charles, Louisiana. He brings a wealth of experience and dedication to his multifaceted life experiences. In a journey spanning over five decades, he has not only served as pastor in both Louisiana and Texas but also served as a Co-Owner of Resource Management Services—a leading Mental Health Rehab provider serving the needs of the seriously Mentally Ill. In his tenure there for 30 years, Dr. Burke served as a counselor and case manager, providing holistic care for those facing Mental Health challenges.

Dr. Burke graduated from McNeese State University with a degree in Speech Education. He also graduated from Southwestern Baptist Theological Seminary with a Masters of Religious Education degree. He later received his Doctorate of Bible Theology from the International Bible Institute and Seminary.

Dr. Burke is married to June Watkins Burke. Together, they have two daughters and six granddaughters. He now devotes his time to writing and sharing the gospel whenever and wherever he can.

Table of Contents

Introduction

One cannot read the scripture without concluding that God has one great desire, and that is to reveal himself to his creation. This great God, whose glory is so overwhelming that we cannot look on him and live, wants us to know him. He wants us to have a personal relationship with him. This study attempts to examine the remarkable account of God's revelation to the world. The fullness of this desire is seen in the coming of Jesus Christ. Those men who followed Jesus and later wrote our New Testament declare over and over that they **BEHELD THE GLORY OF GOD**. They beheld this glory in the person of Jesus.

This glory now lives in the lives of believers. The church, as the body of Christ, is now the instrument God uses to reveal himself to the world. As believers, it is our collective responsibility to submit to his leadership and obey his word. In doing so, the world will see this Glory in us. They will see it in our behaviors, attitudes, work ethics, and relationships. They will see it in our desires, primarily the desire to serve God, who brought about our salvation.

No matter how much I study the Word of God, I cannot get over being amazed that this glorious God wants to reveal himself to me. In the context of creation, I am nothing, yet God knows me intimately and personally. Every day, I get to behold the wonder of this relationship, the wonder of this love for me personally.

My prayer is that this book's content will give you a small glimpse of what Paul describes as the MYSTERY OF THE INCARNATION. May it remind you that everything we have with God is amazing. May we never lose the wonder of that simple statement: JESUS LOVES ME, THIS I KNOW, FOR THE BIBLE TELLS ME SO.

Ronnie Burke

Chapter 1
The Purpose of Scripture

1John1:1-3(NLT)

¹ The one who existed from the beginning is the one we have heard and seen. We saw him with our own eyes and touched him with our own hands. He is Jesus Christ, the Word of life.

² This one who is life from God was shown to us, and we have seen him. And now we testify and announce to you that he is the one who is eternal life. He was with the Father, and then he was shown to us.

³ We are telling you about what we ourselves have actually seen and heard so that you may have fellowship with us. And our fellowship is with the Father and with his Son, Jesus Christ.h

The theme of this book is based on the scripture above. Most scholars believe that John is referring to the Transfiguration when he made this statement. John, James, and Peter had the amazing opportunity to see Jesus transfigured so that his body revealed the glory of God shining through Him.

Matthew 17:2-8 describes the experience.

2 He was transfigured before them, and His face shone like the sun, and His garments became as white as light. 3 And behold, Moses and Elijah appeared to them, talking with Him. 4 Peter said to Jesus, "Lord, it is good for us to be here; if You wish, I will make three tabernacles here, one for You, and one for Moses, and one for Elijah." 5 While he was still speaking, a bright cloud overshadowed them, and behold, a voice out of the cloud said, "This is My beloved Son, with whom I am well-pleased; listen to Him!" 6 When the disciples heard *this,* they fell face down to the ground and were terrified. 7 And Jesus came to *them* and touched them and said, "Get up, and do not be afraid." 8 And lifting up their eyes, they saw no one except Jesus Himself alone. (NIV)

That was an unforgettable experience for John and the other disciples. They were so moved by seeing the glory of God shine through Jesus that they did not want to leave. They wanted to stay and build an altar for protracted worship. Not only did they see the glory of God shine through Jesus, they heard the voice of God speak about how pleased He was with His Son. That voice must have been overwhelming because when they heard it, they were terrified. They fell to the ground, unable to look up until Jesus spoke to them.

I love the statement in verse 8. **They looked up and saw Jesus alone.** When the disciples opened their eyes, Moses and Elijah were gone. The glory that shone like the sun diminished. The only person they saw was Jesus. I want to use this verse in the context of the theme of this book. This is all about Jesus.

THE PURPOSE OF ALL SCRIPTURE IS TO REVEAL JESUS

I think about all of the facts and information we would never know if it was not for the scriptures. If John had not recorded this incident, we would never know about the glory of Jesus being visibly manifested to his disciples. But it would not only be this experience; it would be every other experience recorded in the gospels and the rest of the New Testament. `Not only would we not have this information about Jesus, but we would be extremely limited in what we know about God.

Jesus told the woman at the well that **God is Spirit, and those who worship Him must worship Him in spirit and in truth.** God, being a spirit, cannot be seen by any human being. If we did not have the scriptures, the only thing that we could know about God is what we conjure up in our minds. The Psalms says **the heavens declare the glory of God, and the firmament reveals His handiwork.** From this, we know that God is bigger than the universe. We know that he creates the beauty and the wonder of everything we see. But his creation does not reveal anything about His nature and His character.

Just looking and examining creation does not tell us about God's compassion, forgiveness, holiness, and love. It just reveals His power. So, how can we learn about these characteristics of God? We

3

learn about Him through scripture. God inspired the writing of scripture so we could have a greater knowledge of who He is.

The whole purpose of scripture is to reveal all that God is and all he has done on our behalf. The more that we read and study the scripture, the more we see that everything God did for us and to us was done through Jesus. God wants us to know him. He wants us to know him as the Father who loved us, the Son who saved us, and the Holy Spirit who indwells us. It is through the scripture we learn about the nature and essence of God. The scripture reveals:

God as creator

God as judge

God as the sovereign Lord.

God, the savior who became like us and died for us.

God is the Holy Spirit, who moves in us when we are saved and then guides us through life in this world as we make preparations for heaven.

Scripture reveals not only God's desire to reveal Himself but also how he accomplishes this desire. The fullness of his revelation happened when Jesus came into the world. In Jesus's life, teachings, and work, we learn about God's nature, essence, and characteristics.

If Jesus had not come into the world, what we know about God would be limited to just what we see. We look at creation, and we see that he is greater than the universe. We see that he is powerful in all things. But we would know nothing of his thinking and his character. With the coming of Jesus, we are now able to know things about God that we could never know: **his love, grace, mercy, and compassion.** It is through Jesus that we learn God's great desire. He wants us to know him. He wants to reveal himself to us. He wants us to experience his love, his presence, and his power in us and for us.

The fact that God wants to reveal himself to us is amazing when we consider what we are and then consider who and what He is. He is everything, and we are nothing. The more that we study the universe and its size, the more we learn just how little we are. Once we leave our own galaxy, this earth cannot be seen. It is not even a speck on the universal landscape. In consideration of this, it is amazing that the God who created this universe would want to have anything to do with us.

Another amazing revelation is the fact that we can receive this revelation from God. It is miraculous and supernatural that we are given the intellectual ability to know this great God. This capacity to know Him did not come from our own intellectual ability. God is so "other" than us that it is impossible to know Him without His help. If He does not reveal Himself to us, then we will be like the builders of the Tower of Babel in the Old Testament. The people tried to build a tower that would reach up into the heavens, trying to reach God. This story shows just how unable men are to know God without His intervention.

Left to ourselves, the greatness and the glory of God cannot be known. Paul tells us in 1 Corinthians 2 that the natural man does not have the ability to understand the mind and the thinking of God. When an unspiritual man hears the story of Salvation of how God became a man and died on the cross to save us from our sins, he considers that story foolish. The only way for us to have any kind of knowledge of God was for Him to do an extreme, miraculous work not only for Himself in becoming a man, but He also had to do a miraculous work in our minds and our thinking. He had to give us the ability to understand. That ability comes about through personal belief in the Lord Jesus as a savior.

But even more than God having to do something to us, he also had to do something Himself. He had to perform a miraculous act that was so great no one would have thought about it. God had to become a man like us.

If he did not do this, then we would not know him. His glory and his power made him unapproachable by man. He told Moses, no man can look on my face and live. Yet Jesus came, and through Jesus, we were able to see and know God. Through Jesus becoming a man, people were able to touch God, communicate with God, be blessed by God, and be taught how to have a personal relationship with Him. We can read about all of these interactions in the gospels.

All of the gospel writers had one goal, and that was to say that Jesus was God in the flesh.

The gospel is the revelation that Jesus is the Christ.

Imagine how horrible it would be if Jesus came, lived, died, and rose again, and nothing was ever said about it. How horrible it would be if no one wrote about their experiences with Jesus and why they believed He was God in the flesh. We would remain lost. Yes, hope would be available for salvation, but we would know nothing about it. The scriptures are a vital source for us to know about God's revelation of Himself to the world. It is the source that identifies the truth about who Jesus is.

The gospels are not vague about this claim about Jesus. I realize that many say that Jesus is not God in the flesh, that He never claimed to be, and that the New Testament does not teach that doctrine.

Those who make this claim are not honest in their reading of the scripture. Let's look at some of the evidence the gospel gives proving Jesus is God in the flesh.

Jesus possessed all of the attributes and the power of God.

He had the authority to forgive sin.

Mark 2 tells the story of a paralyzed man brought to Jesus by four friends. They had trouble getting to Jesus because of the crowd of people. They were not going to be deterred. They climbed up on the roof and dug a hole in it to lower their friend down in front of Jesus. Mark says that when Jesus saw the paralyzed man, the first thing He said was **Your sins are forgiven.** A group of religious leaders who were following Jesus to gather evidence against Him complained about His forgiving sin. They commented **Only God can forgive sins.** Jesus then proved that He had the authority to forgive sin by healing the man of his paralysis. He told the **So that you may know The Son of Man has authority on earth to forgive sins, He told the paralyzed man rise, pick up your bed and go home.** Immediately, the paralyzed man was healed.

The New Testament lists multiple miracles Jesus performed during His ministry. None of these miracles were random, but all of them had a purpose. He never performed a miracle for entertainment or a show. Some healings were used as a teaching moment or to meet an urgent need. Other times, Jesus healed to prove his identity and His authority as the Son of God.

He is omniscient means he knows all things.

Throughout His ministry, he was able to know the thinking of those who were out to find fault with him. Luke records in his gospel about the healing of a man on the sabbath day. In chapter 6, he says that Jesus was teaching in one of the synagogues, and there was a man in the congregation who had a withered right hand. The scribes and the Pharisees who were there knew that the man with the crippled hand was present. They were either whispering among themselves or were just quietly wondering whether Jesus was going to heal this man on the sabbath day. In verse 6 Luke says, **but He knew their thoughts.** He knew what they were thinking and what they were conspiring to do. Even though He knew they would become angry if He healed this man, it did not matter to Jesus. He used this time of worship to restore a man's ability to work and take care of his family. The religious leaders responded just the way Jesus knew they would. In verse 11, Luke says, **They were filled with fury and discussed with one another what they might do with Jesus.**

He had authority over every kind of disease.

Matthew tells the story of Peter's mother-in-law being sick with a fever. The Bible says that He touched her, and the **fever left her.** To show that she was completely healed, she got up and began to serve Jesus and the others.

Word was spread in the community that Jesus was in the home of Simon Peter. That evening, a crowd of people showed up at Peter's house, and Jesus spent the evening healing them.

Jesus had authority over demons and evil spirits.

Not only were the sick and crippled brought to Jesus while He was at Peter's home, but those who were **oppressed by demons.** Luke says that Jesus not only healed the sick, but **He cast out the spirits with a word.** The gospels are filled with accounts of Jesus casting out demons and delivering people from oppression and even possession by evil spirits. The power of Jesus over these evil spirits was so great that the people were amazed. Luke 4:36 says, **And, they were all amazed and said to one another, "What is this word? For with authority and power he commands the unclean spirits and they come out."**

Jesus had authority over nature.

The 6th chapter of Mark has two accounts of Jesus' power over nature. The first was the feeding of 5000 people with just a few loaves of bread and fish. After feeding the people and collecting the leftovers, Jesus directed His disciples to get into a boat and cross over to the other side of the Lake. He sent them out on their own while He went up into a mountain to pray. The disciples were having difficulty rowing the boat because they were facing strong headwinds. They just weren't making any progress.

It was during that time that Jesus walked on the water. Verse 48 says that the disciples saw Jesus walking on the water, but they did not recognize Him. Mark says that it appeared as though Jesus was going to walk right past them. Why would this passage be here? It is to show that Jesus has no problem with headwinds. He has no difficulty moving against that which resists Him. The disciples were having problems. They weren't making progress at all, but Jesus was just taking a casual stroll against these high winds.

When they recognized Him, He got in the boat with them, and Mark says, **the wind ceased. And they were utterly astounded.**

Jesus had authority and power over death.

Matthew 9: Jesus raises the daughter of Jarius

Luke 7: Jesus stops a funeral procession and raises a young man from the dead while friends and family are taking him to be buried.

John 11: Jesus raises Lazarus from the dead

Matthew 28: Most important of all, Jesus is raised from the dead after being crucified and buried for three days. Jesus said that **He had the authority to lay down His life and the authority to take it back again. (John 10:17)**

John 2:19: **Jesus said, destroy this temple that is made with hands, and within three days, I will build another without hands.** He was referring to his death and then his coming back to life three days after he was killed.

In summary, all of these passages give evidence that Jesus had the same power, characteristics, and attributes as God. The writers of the New Testament letters affirm the truth of this evidence. Paul said in Colossians 2:9 **I say this because all of God lives in Christ fully, even in his life on earth. (Easy Read Version).** Another translation says **All of God lives in Christs body. (Gods Word Translation)**

All of these scriptures and more reveal that Jesus is God in the flesh. Because Jesus came, we can know more about the nature, holiness, love, forgiveness, and grace of God. (Beacon Bible Commentary, Beacon Hill Press of Kansas City, Kansas City, Missouri 1967, pg 350)

It is not only the gospels that reveal Jesus, but the whole Bible speaks about Him.

The gospel of Luke tells the story of two of Jesus' disciples walking on a road, discussing the events of the day. Jesus was raised from the dead, and the women found the stone rolled away from the tomb where Jesus was buried. They looked inside, and He was not there. They reported that and angel appeared to them and told them that Jesus was not in the tomb. He had risen. The angel told the women to go find the disciples and tell them that Jesus was alive. These were the events they were talking about. And the inference of the passage is that they heard all of these things, but they did not understand them.

Jesus joins them on their journey and enters into a conversation about what the Old Testament says about Jesus. Verse 27 states that Jesus started with Moses and then the prophets. He explained that all of the scripture in the Old Testament was about Himself.

(Read Luke 24:25-27)

Then Jesus said to them, "You are such foolish people! You find it so hard to believe all that the prophets wrote in the Scriptures.

²⁶ **Wasn't it clearly predicted by the prophets that the Messiah would have to suffer all these things before entering his time of glory?"**

²⁷ **Then Jesus quoted passages from the writings of Moses and all the prophets, explaining what all the Scriptures said about himself.**

Notice the phrase, "Beginning with Moses." Moses wrote the first five books of the Bible. Jesus taught his traveling companions that Moses talked about His coming. Moses revealed that a Messiah would be born. Consider some of the revelations about Jesus from the Old Testament.

Jesus walked in the garden with Adam and Eve. The sacrifice of Jesus was pictured when animals were killed and their skins were used to make clothes for Adam and Eve. This portrayed the death of Christ so that lost sinners could receive the spiritual clothing from the Lord and to have the shed blood cover our sins.

It was Jesus who had a meal with Abraham In Genesis 18.

It was Jesus who appeared before Joshua as the Captain of the Army of the Lord in Joshua 5.

When the Hebrews needed water in the desert, Moses struck a rock, and water came out to take care of the needs of the people. According to Paul, this rock that gave water is a picture of Jesus, who provides the water of life for all of us. (Exodus 17)

He is the single door to the Ark that Noah built. The Bible says that Noah built an ark that had one door. There was only one entrance that provided security and life from the judgment that was coming. This one door is a picture of Jesus being the one way to salvation. He is the one way to eternal life. Jesus even referred to this when he said **I am the door. No one comes to the Father except through me.**

He is pictured as the pure lamb offered as a sacrifice on the altar of the Tabernacle and the temple. (Leviticus 1-2)

He is the scapegoat that carries away the sins of the people. (Leviticus 16)

He is Emmanuel, God with us. (Isaiah 7:14)

Most commentators call these experiences **Pre-incarnate appearances or shadows of Jesus found in the Old Testament.** Jesus was making the point to these two disciples that all of the scriptures prophesied about Him and taught about Him.

THE SCRIPTURE NOT ONLY GIVES THE REVELATION OF GOD, BUT IT ALSO GIVES THE REVELATION OF OURSELVES.

The more we see and understand God, the more we understand ourselves. As the Word reveals God, it also reveals us as the contradiction of God or the complete opposite of God.

The scripture reveals that God is holy and we are unholy.

God is good, and all of our best works are like filthy rags.

God is powerful, and we are weak.

God is all-knowing, and we are ignorant.

God is righteous, and we are unrighteous.

God is perfect, and we are sinful.

When we look through the scriptures, we see how far from God and how unlike God we are. It is laughable for any human being to have pride or arrogance when it comes to God. It is humorous to think that we have the ability to understand God and know him apart from his revelation.

At the same time, men claiming that he does not exist because they don't see him shows just how small we are. It would be like an ant crawling on the bottom of our shoe and then reporting back to the ant colony that there is no such thing as a human being.

The scripture reveals that God is in control of all things; even the most insignificant detail of our lives falls under the control of God. Because he is God, there are events and circumstances that he causes that bring pain to us. It is not that God is punishing us or that he is sadistic and enjoys seeing us hurt or suffering. No, God brings events into our lives or allows events to come into our lives because he wants good things for us. He wants to reveal something of himself through those events. We may not understand what he is doing at the time or why, but our faith reminds us that God is good and he is doing good to us and for us.

When difficult things happen, the first thing that we tend to ask is, why? Why did these events happen? Why did I lose my job? Why did God allow my spouse to die? We all have events that we don't understand. We all have circumstances brought on our lives by the will of God that we don't comprehend. We ask questions of the Lord, but he does not always answer us at the time we ask him. Sometimes, the Lord answers our questions, but then, sometimes, he does not.

Many people become angry at what God does or what he allows to happen, but the real question is: how does an imperfect, corrupt mind fully understand the perfect mind of God? We do not have the ability to understand his perfect work and will. We may ask why and we may verbalize our questions, but the mind of God is so far beyond us that the only thing we can understand is what he allows us to understand. The only thing that we are able to see is what he allows us to see.

The Bible gives us an example of this revealing work of God.

Luke 24:13-31 (NLT)

13 That same day, two of Jesus' followers were walking to the village of Emmaus, seven miles out of Jerusalem.

14 As they walked along, they were talking about everything that had happened.

15 Suddenly, Jesus himself came along and joined them and began walking beside them.

16 But they didn't know who he was because God kept them from recognizing him.

17 "You seem to be in a deep discussion about something," he said. "What are you so concerned about?" They stopped short, sadness written across their faces.

¹⁸ Then one of them, Cleopas, replied, "You must be the only person in Jerusalem who hasn't heard about all the things that have happened there the last few days."

¹⁹ "What things?" Jesus asked. "The things that happened to Jesus, the man from Nazareth," they said. "He was a prophet who did wonderful miracles. He was a mighty teacher, highly regarded by both God and all the people.

²⁰ But our leading priests and other religious leaders arrested him and handed him over to be condemned to death, and they crucified him.

²¹ We had thought he was the Messiah who had come to rescue Israel. That all happened three days ago.

²² Then, some women from our group of his followers were at his tomb early this morning, and they came back with an amazing report.

²³ They said his body was missing, and they had seen angels who told them Jesus is alive!

²⁴ Some of our men ran out to see, and sure enough, Jesus' body was gone, just as the women had said."

²⁵ Then Jesus said to them, "You are such foolish people! You find it so hard to believe all that the prophets wrote in the Scriptures.

²⁶ Wasn't it clearly predicted by the prophets that the Messiah would have to suffer all these things before entering his time of glory?"

²⁷ Then Jesus quoted passages from the writings of Moses and all the prophets, explaining what all the Scriptures said about himself.

²⁸ By this time, they were nearing Emmaus and the end of their journey. Jesus would have gone on,

²⁹ but they begged him to stay the night with them, since it was getting late. So he went home with them.

³⁰ As they sat down to eat, he took a small loaf of bread, asked God's blessing on it, broke it, and then gave it to them.

³¹ Suddenly, their eyes were opened, and they recognized him. And at that moment, he disappeared!

These men walked with Jesus for several hours and did not recognize who he was. It was not until the very end of this experience that they recognized him. At the beginning of their conversation, Jesus did not allow them to recognize him. It was not until the end of the day that "their eyes were open." It was then that they recognized him. You might ask how could a disciple of Jesus walk with him and talk with him for hours and not know who he was. This is possible because God made that happen. God kept them from recognizing Jesus, and then it was God who opened their eyes to see him and know who he was. If God had not done that, these disciples would have never recognized him.

This Biblical example teaches us that in our relationship to Jesus, there are going to be times when things happen to us that we will not understand. The reason we will not understand them is because God chooses not to explain them to us at that time. He may choose a later time to reveal some truth to us, or he may not do it at all. The point is that it is God who determines what we know and what we don't know about himself, his word, his will, and his work.

This is what it means to walk by faith. It is a trust that understands that everything God does is within his perfect plan and will. Everything that God does is right and good. We may not know how it is right and good, but because our faith tells us that God is good and never does anything wrong, we trust him even though we don't understand him.

A good example of not understanding the mind and the will of God is the recent events of floods, tornadoes, and loss of life and property. Why did those tornadoes hit the areas that they did? Why did the flooding take place where it happened? Why was one home spared and another destroyed? Why was one life taken and another spared? These are some of those things that remind us that we cannot understand the mind or the works of God. We, by faith, only know that he has a perfect plan. We can only respond to that perfect plan with faith and obedience.

We must remember that God reveals himself to man at a place and time of His choosing. Man cannot dictate how or when God reveals himself. We cannot find, reach, or know God through any efforts of our own. God has to act, or else we would know nothing about him.

The Bible is full of examples of God revealing himself to men. Men like Noah, Abraham, Moses, Paul, and all the disciples. These men, like us, did not have the ability to find God or to know him. If God did not reveal himself to these men they would have spent their lives not knowing anything about him. Abraham would have stayed in his hometown and never traveled to the promised Land. Paul would have remained an angry zealot who hated Christians. The disciples would have remained fishermen, zealots, or tax collectors. They would have gone on with their lives, not knowing that there was anything better for them. But something happened that changed their lives. It was not something that they did, but it was something that God did. He revealed himself to them, and that revelation changed their lives.

God must not only reveal himself, but he must also reveal his plan.

We do not have the intellectual capacity to understand the mind of God. We don't know why he does what he does. For instance, God told Abraham to sacrifice his son Isaac, but God did not explain that command. He just told Abraham to get Isaac and go to a particular place and then kill him. God did not tell Abraham that this was a test. He did not tell Abraham that he had a plan for another sacrifice. He just told Abraham to do it. It was after Abraham lifted the knife to kill his son that God intervened and told him what the reason was.

Joseph is another example of one who did not know the plan or the will of God. Joseph had dreams that God had something great in store for him, but God did not tell Joseph that his rise to greatness was going to be through betrayal, suffering, imprisonment, and heartache. He allowed Joseph to be sold into slavery, and it was not until years later that Joseph realized the plan of God. When Joseph met his brothers during a famine, he told them that **what you meant**

for evil, God meant for good. Joseph did not know how his life was going to end up. He just trusted God for he knew that all God did was right.

And then one other example is when Jesus knelt down and washed the disciple's feet: when He came to Peter, Peter said, "Lord you will not wash my feet." Peter could not believe that Jesus would bend down and wash his feet. Even with all of his failings, Peter had a small understanding that Jesus was the Son of the Living God. So why should the Son of the Living God stoop down and wash his feet? Peter didn't understand this act. Jesus then said something very important. He told Peter, **you don't know what I am doing now, but later on you will.** Jesus was letting him know that God would reveal the reason for this at a later time.

This happens to all believers at some time or another. We know that God is fully in control, and things happen that we don't understand. God may choose to give us a reason and an explanation for it and he may not. But if we are going to know anything about the plan and the work of God, it is when he determines to reveal it to us. God must reveal his plan, and then he must also reveal the explanation or the reason for his plan. If he did not, then we would not know his intent.

We are very presumptuous if we think that we can know what God wants or be able to interpret his will without his direct revelation. We are foolish to think that we can predict what God will do or even cause God to do something just by using certain phrases and words.

Therefore, it becomes sinful for anyone to make demands of God or to use the scripture as some kind of magical word to get God to do something. We do not have that kind of ability with him. He does not give us that. It makes some of the television preaching frivolous and insincere. To say that we can make demands of God, to say that God must do something because we say it or because we quote some scripture, shows immature thinking. We have no power over God to make him do anything. We have no power to know anything that God does not want us to know. He determines what we know and when we know it.

THE SCRIPTURE REVEALS THE DEBT WE OWE TO GOD

As we stated earlier, the more we know about God, the more we learn of ourselves. The scripture teaches that we are indebted to God because of our sins. We either have to pay for our sins ourselves, or we pay through another. The only payment we can make for our sins is eternal separation from God. We don't have the ability to make any kind of acceptable restitution or payment for our sins. The only thing we are capable of doing is adding to our guilt and our debt. We add to our guilt because we cannot stop sinning. No other person can intervene for us because everyone else is guilty themselves and adding to their own personal guilt. Every person is in debt to God. If we are going to be free from our debt, then someone else is going to have to pay for it.

Karl Barth said *So then how does a man get his sins paid for? God had to send someone who was a man and, at the same time, stronger than man. He had to send the God-man, not someone who was half God and half man, but someone who was fully God as though he was not man and fully man as though he was not God.*

He had to be fully man because he was going to have to pay for sin while being sinless. He was going to have to be a man who was not in debt to God for sinful living. At the same time, this person was going to have to be God who, in the power of God, receives the wrath of God. And then, in the power of God, restore us to life and righteousness. (Church Dogmatics: The Doctrine of the Word of God, Part 2. Karl Barth. Hendrickson Publishing, Marketing LLC. 2012)

Paul, through the Holy Spirit, reveals how our debt is paid for. Our debt is canceled through justification. In Romans 3:21, he says that we are **justified as a gift of his grace through the redemption that is in Christ Jesus.** The word justified means **to be declared NOT GUILTY.** When God justifies us, he then sees us as someone who never sinned. How is this possible? How can God overlook or not see our sins? The scripture says that he does it through the death or the sacrifice of Jesus. Because Jesus died on the cross for us, God declares us not guilty through Jesus.

The miracle of justification is the same miracle that we read about in the creation account. Genesis 1 gives the account of God speaking creation into existence. The Bible says that God spoke, and something happened—something was created. The world was formed, and life came into being. The writer, John, explains who was responsible for that creation.

In **John 1:1-3** he says, **¹ In the beginning, the Word already existed. He was with God, and he was God.**

² He was in the beginning with God.

³ He created everything there is. Nothing exists that he didn't make.

Everything that was made in the beginning did not exist. There was nothing remade or recycled. It was new, created out of nothing. Jesus, who is the Word, created all things. Nothing was created without him.

Now, let us look at another creation.

2 Corinthians 5:17 (NKJV)

¹⁷ Therefore, if anyone *is* in Christ, *he is* a new creation; old things have passed away; behold, all things have become new.

This verse says that we are a new creation or a new creature because we are in Christ. So, when Paul says that we are declared not guilty, the reason for that is because we are a new creation. We are a creation that did not exist before we accepted Christ as our savior. Just as the creation of the world in the beginning of time did not come into existence apart from Christ; so the new creation that we have been made also did not come into existence without Christ. God is able to justify us (declare us not guilty) because we are a new creation in Christ.

Because we are a new creation in Christ, we are able to experience the following:

Creative power of God: John 1:1-3

His healing power   Acts 4:18

His saving power   Romans 10:9

Because we have been justified through the creative work of Jesus, we can experience an eternal relationship with God where he continues to reveal himself to us. God declares us not guilty of sin because of the price Jesus paid and that declaration gives him the freedom to have a personal intimate relationship with us. We then begin to experience the joy of discovering the depths of the riches of God's love, grace, mercy and holiness.

Chapter 2
The Purpose of Scripture Part II

In Colossians 3:11, Paul proclaims, **Christ is all and in all.** This concise declaration encapsulates the all-encompassing nature of who Jesus is. Christ is the fullness of all God's intentions for the world. He is the complete embodiment of salvation, leaving no aspect untouched. As one commentary beautifully puts it, "He is the entirety of salvation for his people." (John Gill Commentary on Colossians.)

He is the fullness of forgiveness. Something supernatural and wonderful happens when Jesus forgives us of our sins. All of our forgiven sins are removed from the memory of God. I really cannot explain how an all-knowing God can forget anything, but according to the scripture, He casts all of sins as far as the East is from the West. In another passage, Jesus said that all of our sins are thrown into the depths of the ocean. In some mysterious way, God forgets our sins. This means that God will never bring to our minds the past sins we have been forgiven of. He will never punish us for sins that have been forgiven. He is the fullness of our forgiveness. It is only through His forgiveness that we can have eternal life.

He is possessed with all spiritual blessings for those who believe in Him. He is the source of all the light we need to live in this dark world. He is the source of all the wisdom and knowledge we need to know Him and our Heavenly Father. He is the source of all righteousness. We have no righteousness of our own, but when he comes into our lives, He fills us with His righteousness. He is the source of all our sanctification. This means He is the source of all we need to live a life separated to the Lord. He is the source of all we need to live differently from those who do not know Him as our savior, enriching and fulfilling our lives.

Not only is He the fullness of all things, but Paul says He is in all. Paul means here that Christ is in all things. It speaks of his presence being near us and in us. He is present in every worship service we attend. He promised that when two or three are gathered in His name, he is there with them. He told his disciples before he ascended into heaven that he would be with them until the end of the age. He also promised that He would never leave us or forsake us. There is no place that we can go where we are outside of his presence. There are no circumstances that we ever have to face alone. He is in every hospital room where someone is facing a life-threatening illness. He is present at every wedding ceremony as the bride and groom confess their love and make lifetime commitments of faithfulness. He is in every funeral service as loved ones say goodbye to those who have gone on. There is no place where He is not. His presence fills that place, so there is nothing outside of his vision or his understanding of what is happening.

According to John Gill, the Arabic version of this passage is translated as **Christ is above all and in all.**

The primary purpose of scripture is to prove the truth of this Statement. To be all in all speaks about time and eternity. Jesus addresses the concept of time and eternity when he says, **"I am the alpha and omega, the beginning and the end."** Even though it is not stated, it is inferred that He is present not only at the beginning and the end of all things but also everything in between. Paul defines in more detail what he means when he says that Christ is all and in all In Colossians 1:16-20.

<u>16</u> **For by Him all things were created, *both* in the heavens and on earth, visible and invisible, whether thrones or dominions or rulers or authorities—all things have been created through Him and for Him. <u>17</u> He is before all things, and in Him all things hold together. <u>18</u> He is also head of the body, the church, and He is the beginning, the firstborn from the dead, so that He Himself will come to have first place in everything. <u>19</u> For it was the *Father's* good pleasure for all the fullness to dwell in Him, <u>20</u> and through Him to reconcile all things to Himself, having made peace through the blood of His cross; through Him, *I say,* whether things on earth or things in heaven.**

All things are created by Him (1:16)

All things are held together by Him (1:17)

All the fullness of God is in Him (1:19)

All things are reconciled to Him. (1:20)

And then in Colossians 2:3, Paul says **All the treasures of wisdom and knowledge are in him.** This passage and others teach that if we truly desire a more profound knowledge of God, we can learn about Him by studying the life of Jesus. The more we know Jesus, the more we know about God the Father.

The Old Testament is described as the age of prophecy about Christ. It prophesied where He would be born, the kind of life He would live, and his death. Now that He has fulfilled all scripture in the Old Testament, We entered into a new age. Where the Old Testament was the age of prophecy about Jesus, those living in the time after His death, resurrection, and ascension are living in the age of witness. We are living in a time when we give witness to the truth of what the scripture says about Jesus. It is the truth that says:

He has a name that is above all other names.

There is salvation in no other.

One day, every knee will bow, and every mouth will confess the truth that he is Lord.

He has a dwelling place in our lives that no one else could achieve. Christ is in us. The fullness of His life is in us.

Those of us who are believers now have the same job that the writers of the New Testament had, and that was to prove that Jesus is God in the flesh. 1 John 1:2 says **the life was manifested, and we have seven and bear witness and declare to you that eternal life which was with the Father and was manifested to us**. John says that he and the other disciples walked with Jesus during His ministry and are witnesses to all of the events that prove He is the Son of God.

They were witness to His life of miracles and teaching.

They were witness to His death on the cross.

They were witness to His resurrection as He appeared to them at various times.

They were witness to His ascension into Heaven.

They witnessed the arrival of the Holy Spirit, which empowered them to preach, teach, and live the gospel.

We are now the ones who bear witness to the truth of who Jesus is. The question is, "How do we do that?" We were not there to witness the events that John is referring to. So how do we bear witness to the truth Jesus is God in the flesh? We bear witness through the experiences of our lives. We know what happened when we opened our hearts to Jesus. We were separated from God, and now we are part of the family of God. As one line used in the series THE CHOSEN," I Was one way, and now I'm not." What a great witness. I was once lost, but now I am found. I was once blind, but now I see. I was once alone, but now I am filled with the presence of the living Lord. I know that He is alive because He lives in me. We bear witness to the life of Jesus by the change He made in us. He makes us like Him. We love others because He loved others. We forgive those who offend us because Jesus forgives others of their sins. We show grace, mercy, and compassion because Jesus lives in us, and he expresses these qualities through us.

I've come across countless testimonies from believers who have undergone a radical transformation in their lives. Abusive men became loving husbands. Rebellious children became obedient and respectful to their parents. Some who were addicted to drugs became clean. The alcoholic became sober. Some people have shared that their friends notice these changes and want to know what happened to them. They then have the chance to tell them of the change that took place because they received Jesus as their savior. These are some of the ways that we bear witness to the living Lord.

We also bear witness to the fact that without Jesus, nothing would have real meaning or significance. The theological principles of the Bible have no meaning apart from Jesus. Wisdom, righteousness, sanctification, and redemption have no relevance apart from Jesus. The Sermon on the Mount offers good ethical teachings, but without Christ, it is impossible to follow or do. For instance, how does someone turn the other cheek without the help of Jesus? How does one go a second mile without the help and strength of Jesus?

Most important of all is that there would be no hope of eternity if Jesus was not God. There would be no one preparing a place for those who are believers. Heaven would not be possible because we would remain in our sin. If Jesus is not God, then there would be no anticipation of a second coming. Those of us who are believers are looking forward to the day when the trumpet will sound, the dead in Christ will rise, and He who is Lord of Lords and King of Kings comes and takes his children to a place prepared for us. If Jesus is not God, then all of that would be nothing more than wishful thinking. If Jesus is not God, then the New Testament is nothing more than a religious history book about the Hebrew people. There would be no Christianity, no church, no chosen people of God. If Jesus is not God, then all of these things that I just mentioned would be meaningless. But, praise God, all of these things have special meaning and significance because Jesus is God.

Our witness as believers has the same purpose as the first disciples, and that is to declare that Jesus is God in the flesh. Our witness is the declaration that Jesus is God. We give witness to his birth, His life, His death, and His resurrection. We tell the same story that Peter, James, John, Paul, and all the other early believers told. We get to tell how Jesus invaded our lives and radically changed us. We bear witness that there is no one before Him, and no one will come after Him who can compare to His glory. Our witness says:

He has a name that is above all other names.

He provides salvation that no one else can give.

He makes new creatures out of everyone who believes in Him as a savior.

He is coming again, and on that day, every knee will bow, and every tongue will confess that this Jesus who lived in history is Lord, Lord, and King of Kings.

JESUS WAS FULLY GOD AND AT THE SAME TIME FULLY MAN AS IF HE WAS NOT GOD.

The previous statement is a mystery that we really don't have the ability to comprehend. Jesus was not part God and part man. He was the GOD MAN. As we stated previously, and we will state multiple times again, God became a man so He could pay the price for our sins and provide everlasting life for us.

God becoming a man was not a new concept when Jesus came. The world had many mythical stories of how gods became men. The problem is that in the world of mythology, the gods who became men had the characteristics of men. They became jealous, demonstrated uncontrollable anger, and were vengeful and spiteful. The difference between Jesus and these mythological gods is that He never developed sinful human characteristics. He never had uncontrollable rage, a spirit of vengeance, or jealousy. Jesus never had these attitudes or emotions.

When Jesus came as a man, He lived His life the way God intended for men to live. Jesus was the example of what God wanted for us. Jesus lived a life that God desired for all of us to live. He lived in complete obedience and submission to the Father. He was always showing the love of God to those who were considered to be worthless or insignificant to others. He lived a life of unselfish love for others, no matter their station or social status in life. He loved men and women so much that He was willing to sacrifice Himself so we could spend eternity in heaven. He was the GOD MAN.

THE KNOWLEDGE OF JESUS BEING GOD DID NOT COME IMMEDIATELY. IT WAS A KNOWLEDGE THAT DEVELOPED OVER TIME.

The understanding that Jesus was more than just an ordinary man did not come from the disciples themselves. This was not some piece of revelation they figured out for themselves. God revealed this to them through the time they spent with Jesus. When the disciples first met Jesus, they considered Him to be the Messiah, but not God. They considered Him to be a great teacher but not God. Everyone who followed Him did not follow Him because they thought He was God. They thought he was a prophet, John the Baptist, or some other religious figure. When Jesus was alone with His disciples, He asked them what other people thought about Him. Who did they think He was?

Matthew 16:13=19

13 **Now, when Jesus came into the district of Caesarea Philippi, He was asking His disciples, "Who do people say that the Son of Man is?" 14 And they said, "Some** *say* **John the Baptist; and others, Elijah; but still others, Jeremiah, or one of the prophets." 15 He said to them, "But who do you say that I am?" 16 Simon Peter answered, "You are the Christ, the Son of the living God." 17 And Jesus said to him, "Blessed are you, Simon Barjona, because flesh and blood did not reveal** *this* **to you, but My Father who is in heaven. 18 "I also say to you that you are Peter, and upon this rock, I will build My church, and the gates of Hades will not overpower it. 19 "I will give you the keys of the kingdom of heaven, and whatever you bind on earth shall have been bound in heaven, and whatever you loose on earth shall have been loosed in heaven." 20 Then He warned the disciples that they should tell no one that He was the Christ. (NIV)**

Up until this point in Jesus' ministry, people who followed Him and listened to Him did not grasp the reality of who He really was. Jesus then asked His disciples. Peter immediately responded that Jesus was the Christ, the Son of the living God. This answer given by Peter showed a deeper understanding of who Jesus was. Notice how this information came to Peter. It did not come because of his own thinking or by his own dedication. No. Jesus informed Peter about the source of this information. This information was given to Peter by the Father in heaven. God revealed this truth to Peter. Just as God revealed this same truth on the Mount of Transfiguration when He spoke and said, this is my son. Men and women, on their own, are not able to grasp this great mystery. You and I are not able to grasp the truth of this on our own. We needed help to understand who Jesus fully is. God had to do to us the same thing He did do Peter. God has to give us understanding so we can believe. God had to give us faith that everything we read about Him in the Bible is true. And it is God who lets us know that unless we believe in Jesus, we can never experience heaven.

The journey to understanding that Jesus was the Son of God started with the belief in Jesus as a man. They did not see divinity in

Jesus at first. Their concept of a Messiah was not one who would deliver them from the power of sin but someone who would deliver them from the power of Rome. They believed that the Messiah Moses prophesied about was going to be a king who would set up a kingdom with Jerusalem as the capital. They anticipated a military figure who would overcome all enemies.

This understanding is recorded in the rest of the story in Matthew 16. After Peter confessed that Jesus was the Christ, the son of the living God, Jesus began to talk about His coming death. He told His disciples about dying at the hands of the religious leaders. When he was speaking, Peter interrupted Him. Peter could not accept what Jesus was saying. Matthew says that **Peter took Jesus aside and began to rebuke Him, saying, God forbid it, Lord, this can never happen.** (Matthew 16:22) Why would Peter passionately rebuke Jesus for talking about His death? It is because Peters's concept of the Messiah was political, military, and social. It was not spiritual. In Peter's mind, If Jesus was truly the Messiah, then He couldn't die.

In Peter's mind, the Messiah could not be beaten by any enemy. He would overcome all oppressors. Here was a man who could raise an army that would be impossible to beat. If soldiers were killed, He could just raise them from the dead. If they ran out of food, He could feed them with a minuscule lunch. They would never suffer exhaustion because he would strengthen and empower them. No one could stand against Him.

Peter's thinking and understanding of the Messiah were not uncommon. This is what most Jews thought. None of them understood that the power of Jesus was not going to be revealed through armies and battles, but it would be revealed in the hearts and minds of all those who believed. So, for Jesus to talk about dying was not acceptable to the disciples.

JESUS SPENT THREE YEARS IN MINISTRY, TEACHING THAT HIS MISSION WAS A SPIRITUAL ONE, NOT A POLITICAL ONE.

He continued to identify Himself in spiritual terms. Look at how He identifies Himself.

I am the bread of life. (John 6:18)

I am the light of the world. (John 10:7)

I am the door of the sheep (John 11:26)

I am the way the truth and the life. (John 14:3)

I am the true vine. (John 15:1)

I am the Alpha and Omega, the beginning and the end. (Revelation 1:8)

All the way to the end of the Lord's ministry, the disciples were thinking in terms of a political kingdom and now a spiritual one. This is the reason the disciples were shocked when the soldiers came to arrest Jesus in the Garden of Gethsemane. This could be the reason Peter took a sword and swung it at the head of the servant of the High Priest. Maybe if he would fight, then Jesus would fight back. It is believed by some that the primary reason Judas betrayed Jesus was because He wanted to force Jesus to begin the revolution that was expected. When the soldiers came to arrest Jesus, Judas may have thought that Jesus would not surrender to them and He would fight back. When Jesus did not, Judas realized that Jesus never intended to start a physical revolution. It was then He went to the priest and said, I **have betrayed an innocent man**. (Matthew 27:3-5)

It wasn't until after the resurrection that the disciples realized Jesus was more than just a man. When Thomas saw Jesus after the resurrection, He exclaimed **my Lord and my God.** (John 20:28). At that moment, Jesus was more than just a great teacher, miracle worker, and healer. He was God.

WHY IS IT IMPORTANT TO CONFESS JESUS AS LORD (GOD)

We've spent a lot of time emphasizing that Jesus was man and, at the same time, He was God. Who He is must be believed before a person can become a Christian. A person cannot become a Christian if he only believes in the historical Jesus who came, taught, and worked miracles. Many great men in history have done some of these things, but none of them were God. In the other religions of the world, none of their leaders make that claim. Mohammed, Buddha, Confucius, or any other cult leader made that claim. An individual can believe in the life and teachings of all these other religious leaders, but that belief does not give them eternal life. It is the confession of Jesus as Lord God brings salvation.

For if you confess with your mouth that Jesus is Lord and believe in your heart that God raised Him from the dead, you will be saved. For it is believing in your heart that you are made right with God, and it IS BY CONFESSING WITH YOUR MOUTH THAT YOU ARE SAVED. (Romans 10:9-10. NLT)

This belief and confession are not optional. It is not a choice that we have. We either believe and confess that Jesus is God, or we remain lost and separated from God forever.

Romans 10:12-13 says, As the scriptures tell us, **"Anyone who believes in Him will not be disappointed." Gentile Jews and Gentiles are the same in this respect. They all have the same Lord, who generously gives his riches to all who ask for them. Anyone who calls on the name of the Lord will be saved**. (NLT). This passage makes it clear that the only way a person can be saved is through the confession of Jesus as Lord. Paul makes the point that this confession is the same for the Jews and the Gentiles. I have listened to some very popular preachers who say that the Jews do not have to be evangelized because they are already to chosen people of God. If this is true then that means there are two paths to salvation. The first path is by being born a Jew. The second path is that if you are not a Jew, then you must confess that Jesus is Lord. The theology of dual paths to salvation is not found in scripture. Jesus made it clear that No one could come to the Father except through Him.

This also means that there cannot be divided beliefs in spiritual matters. What I mean by this is that if someone is brought up in another religion, such as Islam, Buddhism, or other kind of faith, they must give up that faith in order to be able to receive salvation. Becoming a Christian is the result of exclusive belief and commitment to Jesus and Jesus alone. It is more than just believing; it is confessing the truth of who Jesus is. He is the Lord God who became a man.

Right now, Confessing Jesus as Lord is optional for everyone. Each person who hears the story of Jesus decides whether or not they are going to believe. They can choose whether they are going to confess Christ or not. However, there is coming a time, when the confession of the Lordship of Christ is not going to be optional. Paul says that when Jesus returns, every person, no matter who they are, what religion they belong to or whatever belief system they have, is going to confess Jesus.

Philippians 2:9-11 says **Because of this, God raised him up to the heights of heaven and gave him a name that is above every other name, that at the name of Jesus, every knee will bow, in heaven and on earth and under the earth. EVERY TONGUE WILL CONFESS THAT JESUS CHRIST IS LORD, TO THE GLORY OF GOD THE FATHER.**

Chapter 3
The Mystery of the Incarnation

The miracle of all miracles is that God became a man. The Bible calls this event THE MYSTERY OF THE INCARNATION. There are so many unexplainable factors in the coming of Jesus that we don't have the ability to understand them all, but we are asked by the Father to believe them.

The first part of the mystery is that when Jesus became a human being, he was equal to us in every way. This means that no human experience was excluded from His life. He felt hunger, sadness, and grief, became tired, and experienced thirst. He felt the grief of losing Joseph, his earthly father. He experienced disappointment with his disciples when they argued among themselves about who was going to be the greatest in the kingdom.

These are the physical and emotional experiences Jesus had, but there were also spiritual experiences He went through as well.

He had to be born under the Law. He became responsible for obeying the Law of God. The fact that he kept that Law and did not sin made it possible for Jesus to become our savior.

He experienced temptation throughout his life and ministry. The Bible says **There is no temptation common to man that our Lord did not face**. (I Corinthians 10:13. NLT). In our day and age, we think that there are temptations that we face today that Jesus did not face when He was here, but that is not true. Sin has been the same since Adam and Eve disobeyed God in the Garden of Eden. No matter what age in History or whatever generation is living, there is no new sin. The writer of Ecclesiastes says, **what has been is what will be, and what has been done is what will be done, and there is nothing new under the sun**. (Ecclesiastes 1:9 MRSV). The same sins and kinds of sins we face today are the same kinds of sins that have been around since the beginning of time. Therefore it is true that Jesus faced the same temptations, we face in our generation. Even though Jesus faced serious temptations, He never gave in. He remained faithful to His Father and did not commit one sin. He never committed a sin of action where he did something he should not have done. He never committed sins of the mind. He never thought about doing anything that would dishonor His Father. He never committed any kind of emotional sins such as anger, rage, jealousy, or others. HE NEVER SINNED. He was perfect in every area of His life. That in itself is a mystery. How could Jesus live in a family with siblings and never sin? How could He live in a family and never do anything that was wrong or say anything that was sinful? He could only do this because He was the God-Man.

As each disciple wrote their gospels, they reflected on their experiences with Jesus. They remembered how He lived His life. They thought about how He never did anything wrong, broke any law of God, and was righteous and holy all through his life. When these men gave testimony of their relationship to Jesus, they did not say, "We have found a great man" or "We discovered a great teacher." No, they said none of these things. Instead, to a man, they all said the same thing. **WE HAVE FOUND THE CHRIST. WE HAVE FOUND THE SON OF GOD, AND WE HAVE HEARD HIS WORD.** The relationship they had with Jesus was to experience the presence of God and His word.

Each of the gospels begins with Jesus of Nazareth, but they conclude their gospel with Jesus, the Son of God, who has risen from the dead. It was in the experience of the resurrection that they were able to look back at his life, ministry and teaching. When they looked at the life of Jesus through the lens of the resurrection, they could say, "Now I understand."

The resurrection and the coming of the Holy Spirit are the critical point of their understanding. All through his ministry, He told them of his coming death, burial, and resurrection. Even though He discussed this with them, they were slow to understand. They did not have the spiritual acumen to understand. But when the Holy Spirit came, they not only had an understanding of who Jesus was but they were also empowered to tell everyone they met that Jesus was the Christ, the Son of God.

The resurrection of Jesus is the most critical event in History. If there had been no resurrection, there would be no Messiah. There would be no Christ. There would only be Jesus, the man. The resurrection proves who Jesus claimed to be. As a human, He obeyed the Father in all things. He did not sin. He then paid the price for the sins of everyone. All of this would be nothing more than words about a good story, but the resurrection proves that this was more than someone making a bogus claim about who He was. This was the proof He was God in the flesh.

Jesus is God, but more than that, He is GOD WITH US AND FOR US. He sits at the right hand of the Father in heaven while at the same time living within those who are His believers. Only God can do this.

THE FREEDOM OF GOD TO BE OUR GOD

This sounds like an unusual statement. Isn't God free to do what He wants? After all, He is God. He is not limited by time, space, or intellectual capacity. However, in regard to our own lives, God could not have a personal indwelling relationship with us. The reason He could not was because of the sinfulness and the unholiness of our lives. Because God is Holy and we are not, there was no way that we could enter into His presence. Because of the unholiness of our lives, God could not live within us. A Holy God cannot have anything to do with a sinful, unholy person.

The story in Genesis reveals this separation between God and His creation. When Adam and Eve sinned, the Bible says that they were expelled from the garden. Before they sinned, they were able to have fellowship with God. Genesis 3:8 says, "**And they heard the sound of the LORD God walking in the garden in the cool of the day, and the man and his wife hid themselves from the presence of the LORD God among the trees of the garden**. This simple statement described the kind of relationship they had with God. It was a personal relationship where they could meet with Him and talk with Him. After they sinned against God, they immediately realized that something terrible had happened. We know this because when God called to them, they were hiding. They were ashamed because they sinned against the Lord.

After they appeared before the Lord, they told Him what happened. It was then that the Lord clothed them and then expelled them from the garden. A holy God could not fellowship with unholy, sinful men, so he kicked them out of his presence. From that time until the coming of Jesus, God had a distant relationship with his creation. He had an external relationship with men.

Even though in the Old Testament, God declared Himself to be the God of Abraham, Isaac, and Jacob, this declaration was one of choice to accomplish an eternal purpose. He chose these men for the purpose of creating a nation where the Son of God would be born. Why did He choose Abraham? God could have chosen anyone, but He chose Abraham to be the Father of a new nation, the nation of Israel. Israel was going to be the nation that would bring the savior into the world. He was going to use Israel to bring about the God-Man to deal with the sin problem. Once the sin problem was taken care of, God could have a relationship with us. He could have much more than an external relationship. It was going to be an internal relationship where He lives inside of us. It was going to be a relationship where we who believed in Jesus were going to become THE TEMPLE OF THE HOLY SPIRIT. God was going to be free to save us from our sins, make us His children, and live in us. Jesus, paying for our sins, gave God the freedom to change us and live in us. Karl Barth said, "Not only is God now free to be our God, but we are free to be his people."(Karl Barth, The Doctrine of Reconciliation, Church Dogmatics)

If Jesus had not come, this type of relationship would be impossible. If Jesus had not come, God would have to deal with us as He did in the Old Testament. He would have to deal with us from a distance. None of us could approach Him because of the sin in our lives. With the coming of Jesus, God is:

Our creator

Our Reconciler

Our Redeemer

Because of the coming of Jesus, we now know ourselves as:

A chosen generation

A royal priesthood

A Holy Nation

A people for God's own possession.

Because of Jesus, the fullness and the completeness of our needs are met. We do not have to do anything to please God and gain his acceptance. The Bible is clear that there is nothing we can do to gain God's approval. The only way we can gain God's approval is because of what Jesus did on the cross. His death paid the price for our sins. His blood covered our sins to where God does not see them. Because of the cross, we have eternal life. We also have access to a continuing revelation of God. We have continual forgiveness for our sins and failures. We always have His eternal presence.

Because of the arrival of Jesus, God is the God of the universe, but for the first time, He is God within us and among us. God is able to cross the great divide between us and Himself. The more we think about this, the more we can see just how much God loved us. It is love that explains his condescension towards us. His love for us is something that we cannot explain. There was nothing in us that compelled God to love us the way that He did and provided a way for us to have a relationship with Him.

When asked what he thought was the greatest theological principle, Karl Barth said. "The greatest theological concept is found in the simple song, JESUS LOVES ME THIS I KNOW FOR THE BIBLE TELLS ME SO. (Karl Barth, Recorded Interview concerning his writings)

THE COMING OF JESUS REVEALS THE DEPTHS GOD WENT THROUGH JUST SO WE COULD KNOW HIM.

God revealed Himself in a way that we could tolerate and in a way that we would recognize. If God revealed Himself in the fullness of His glory, then we could not know Him. We would not be able to survive that kind of revelation. God did not reveal Himself as a being or a creature that we would not recognize. He came as one of us. Because He became a man, the invisible God became visible. The untouchable God became touchable. Men, women, and children could approach Him, touch Him, sit in his lap, and anoint Him with oil. To appear in any other way would have made this kind of relationship impossible. God does not meet us as a stranger, but someone we are familiar with. He meets us as a man.

The great mystery is how God could become a man and remain true to Himself, which was fully God and, at the same time, fully man. There was never a moment when He was not God. He was God in the manger. He was God when preaching the Sermon on the Mount. He was God while walking on the water. He was God paying the price for our sins on the cross. He was God who walked out of the tomb.

Martin Luther put it like this:

Whom all the world could not contain

He lies in Mary's' lap

Who all things He does sustain

Has taken an infant nap.

What an amazing thought. The God who is bigger than the universe, whose glory fills the heavens, becomes a baby to save you and me.

Chapter 4
The Glory of God Stepped Into History

When the fullness of time had come, God sent His son, born of a woman and born under the law. (Galatians 4:4. NLT)

Time is something that is measured by our life. It is not something that God measures. In eternity, there is no such thing as time. Time is a measurement of when an event begins and when it ends. For instance, a day begins with sunrise and ends at sunset. All historical events begin with an event and continue until another event begins.

God does not measure time this way.

The Bible speaks about the **fullness of time. (Galatians 4:4).** This is a spiritual indication of the moment God determined to send Jesus. It was the time when God decided everything was ready for the Messiah to come. **"It** is often asked why he did not come sooner, and why mankind did not have the benefit of his incarnation and atonement immediately after the fall? Why were four thousand dark and gloomy years allowed to roll on, and the world suffered to sink deeper and deeper in ignorance and sin? To these questions perhaps no answer entirely satisfactory can be given. God undoubtedly saw reasons which we cannot see and reasons which we shall approve if they are disclosed to us." (Barnes Notes on Galatians, Albert Barnes, Baker Publishing 1983)

There have been many other suggestions by various commentators and to what this term means. Some suggested that God allowed thousands of years to pass so that men would have the opportunity to see that all of their plans for finding God would fail. Since the beginning there have been many religions and cults created for the purpose of finding God or finding a way to heaven. None of these religions gave real hope to anybody. So, after making all kinds of attempts for personal salvation or going to heaven that failed, God sent His son into the world to show that there was only one way to reach Him, and that was through His Son Jesus.

It was also a time of relative peace. Rome ruled the world at that time, and even though it was an oppressive government, it maintained peace in the regions it controlled.

It was a time of oppression and hopelessness. People felt that they had no choice and they definitely did not have any power to change things. There were zealots in Israel who stirred the population to rebel against Rome, only to end in disaster. God sent his son into the world to reveal that an oppressive government cannot keep a person from finding freedom and peace.

It was a time when religion was inefficient and corrupt. The religious leaders were more concerned about their own power rather than helping people find peace with God. They made themselves rich off of the rules and regulations they forced men and women to follow. Jesus was so angry on one of his trips to the temple that he literally overthrew money changers' tables and released animals for sacrifice because of the corruption.

The Passover of the Jews was at hand, and Jesus went up to Jerusalem. In the temple, he found those who were selling oxen and sheep and pigeons and the money changers sitting there. And making a whip of cords, he drove them all out of the temple, with the sheep and oxen. And he poured out the coins of the money changers and overturned their tables. And he told those who sold the pigeons, "Take these things away; do not make my Father's house a house of trade." His disciples remembered that it was written, "Zeal for your house will consume me. (John 2:13-17, ESV)

Jesus said that these religious leaders were so corrupt that when they made converts, they made them **a child of hell.**

But woe to you, scribes and Pharisees, hypocrites! For you shut the kingdom of heaven in people's faces. For you neither enter yourselves nor allow those who would enter to go in. Woe to you, scribes and Pharisees, hypocrites! For you travel across sea and land to make a single proselyte, and when he becomes a proselyte, you make him twice as much a child of hell as yourselves. (Matthew 23:13-15; ESV)

It was in this environment that Jesus came.

The "fullness of time" also describes how the coming of Jesus into the world fills up our lives. The Bible says that before Jesus came, we were empty, lost, and in darkness. When Jesus came, he fills up our emptiness with his fullness. To be lost means that we were lost from God. We were separated from Him because of our sins. When Jesus came, he found us in our lost condition and filled us up with Himself so we could have an eternal relationship with God the Father. He fills our darkness with the light of His life.

So, when Paul speaks about the "fullness of time," it means the fullness of Jesus coming into the world.

In Colossians 3:11, Paul says that Jesus is **the fullness of the Revelation of God. He is the fullness of salvation, and He is the fullness of life.** By coming into the world, Jesus made our time (Our life) complete. Our life is measured by time from birth to death. In our life, Jesus makes us full. In our life, Jesus makes us complete. Because of the fullness and the completeness that Jesus makes in our lives, we are now able to enter into the right relationship with God.

One of the things that we have to learn as a believer is that time with God does not mean the same thing as time with us. We look at time based on our life experiences. There are moments when it seems that time crawls along as we wait for an answer, a diagnosis, a job interview, or an acceptance letter.

Other times, it seems that time moves too quickly, and we are not prepared for what is happening at the moment.

We spend our Christian life learning that God moves according to his own time. We measure time in hours, days, and minutes. God does not have a clock to go by. He does not send an alarm for something to happen. Time with him is far different than time for us. Peter said, **But you must not forget dear friends that a day is like a thousand years to the Lord and a thousand years is like a day. (2 Peter 3:1-10).** Peter was writing this letter just a few years after the ascension of Jesus. The disciples spoke about His return. Peter wrote this letter approximately 30 years after the ascension of Jesus. Those critics who listened to the preaching of the disciples about the second coming of Christ began to mock them because

Jesus had not returned. He said that **there would be scoffers who argue that Jesus promised to return, but where is He. (2 Peter 3:4 NLT).** In their minds, 30 years was plenty of time for the Lord to return. Since He had not come back, it must be nothing but a myth. It was then that Peter explained that God's time is not ours.

We have the same complaint today by those who do not believe in Christ as their personal savior. They argue that "it has been 2000 years since Jesus lived. He said He was coming back. Well, where is He? They believe that since it has been 2000 years, then He is not going to return. Peter's letter explains that Jesus is going to return at the time of His choosing. If we take God's time, as Peter describes in his letter, then it has only been two days since the ascension of Jesus. The Bible describes **our life as a vapor, a mist, or a morning fog.** (James 4:14 NLT). We might live 70 or 100 years, but that length of time is only a moment with God.

The Bible reminds us that we don't have any control over our time. We cannot make it speed up or slow down. We do not have the power to make things happen when we want them to happen. We can't even determine the activities of our life with certainty. James says **Look here, you people who say, "Today or tomorrow we are going to a certain town and will stay there are year. We will do business there and make a profit." How do you know what will happen tomorrow? What you ought to say is, "If the Lord wants us to, we will live and do this or that. Otherwise, you will be boasting about your own plans, and all such boasting is evil. (James 4:13-16 NLT).** We are incapable of determining anything about the time or the activities of our life. God determines everything that happens to us in all the moments of our life.

Jesus told His disciples that **It is not for you to know the times and the seasons. The Lord sets those dates, and they are not for you to know. (Acts 1:6-7 NLT)**

Our time has a beginning and an end. God has no beginning and no end. Also, we must learn that God does not operate or make decisions based on our expectations but according to His will and purpose.

GOD COMING INTO HISTORY IS AN ACT OF LORDSHIP

The purpose of the New Testament is to prove that Jesus is Lord over everything. There is nothing outside of his control and power. He has the power to do what He wants, to who He wants, and when He wants. When we confess that Jesus is the Lord of our lives, we are saying that He is the total and ultimate authority in our lives. By confessing that Jesus is Lord, we confess that we are submitting to His authority over us.

Salvation then, becomes more than just praying a prayer and asking Jesus into our hearts. It is the understanding that we are giving up the rights of our life. We are giving up the right to make decisions for ourselves without submission to God's will for our lives. Being saved is much more than just going to heaven when we die. Being saved is a person who submits to the authority of Christ in every area of HIs life: his home, his job, his recreation, his plans, and his relationship with others. If Jesus is Lord, then he controls all of these areas of our life. When we confess that Jesus is Lord, we are saying that we are now **friends with God.** This friendship could never have happened if God did not become one of us. We would never know Him, find Him, or be able to have a relationship with Him if He had not come. **This great miracle happened because He loved us.**

Chapter 5
His Glory is Eternal

In John 1:14, the writer says that he saw the glory of Jesus, **and it was the glory of the son of God.** Most commentators believe that John is referring to his experience on the Mount of Transfiguration, where the glory of God overshadowed and filled Jesus. The disciples who were with Jesus at that moment were overwhelmed with the sight. It was such a wonderful experience that they did not want to leave. They wanted to stay and built altars for worship.

This is Matthews's record of the event.

2 And He was transfigured before them; and His face shone like the sun, and His garments became as white as light. 3 And behold, Moses and Elijah appeared to them, talking with Him. 4 Peter said to Jesus, "Lord, it is good for us to be here; if You wish, I will make three tabernacles here, one for You, and one for Moses, and one for Elijah." 5 While he was still speaking, a bright cloud overshadowed them, and behold, a voice out of the cloud said, "This is My beloved Son, with whom I am well-pleased; listen to Him!" 6 When the disciples heard *this,* they fell face down to the ground and were terrified. 7 And Jesus came to *them* and touched them and said, "Get up, and do not be afraid." 8 And lifting up their eyes, they saw no one except Jesus Himself alone.

I believe that each of us who are believers had experiences where we were so moved by what God was doing in that moment and the emotional and spiritual experience so touched us that we did not want it to end. We wanted it to keep going. I love Southern gospel music. I have been to concerts of my favorite groups where I did not want it to end. I wanted them to keep singing. It is this kind of feeling the disciples had. Of course, their experience was far greater than anyone we ever experienced. We felt the move of God on our lives and wanted more. John and his friends saw the glory of God shining forth from the body of Jesus on the Mount of Transfiguration they wanted more.

Even though John may be speaking about the transfiguration in this passage, he actually did have many more opportunities to see the glory of Jesus through the preaching, teaching, healing, and other miracles He did. In this study I want us to see that the glory of Jesus had more to do than just the experience on the mountain. The glory of Jesus was witnessed throughout his life. I also want us to see how the glory of Jesus is now in us and He wants to reveal His glory through us to the world.

However, before the glory of Jesus was revealed in this world, He had greater glory in heaven. Jesus was filled with glory and majesty long before the world began.

Jesus Christ shared in God's majesty before time.

The apostle Paul said **Christ is the visible image of the invisible God. He existed before anything was created and is supreme over all creation. Colossians 1:15 (NLT)**

Notice two important statements in this verse. First, Jesus is the image of God, and second, he is eternal. He existed before the creation of the world. Being in the image of God refers to likeness, authority, and preeminence over everything. It refers to his equality with the Father. Jesus said that **he who has seen me has seen the father. (John 14:9).**

In another passage, Jesus said **I and the Father are one. (John 10:30)**

These passages mean that Jesus is the same as the Father. Paul points out that Jesus is the image of the **invisible God.** This means that by becoming flesh and entering into the world, you have even more wonderful thoughts when we consider this majestic God, who is, above all, limited in what we can see and know about God the Father. With the coming of Jesus, we now have a visible picture of God that we can see, study, and learn about Him. We are unable to see The Father because He is Spirit. But when Jesus came into the world as a man, we can now know what God is like. We can see the character, the love, the grace, and the beauty of God.

Being in the image of God means that Jesus is the same. It means that he is equal to the Father in all things. Therefore, since he is equal to the Father in all things, he shares the majesty of the Father in eternity.

The word majesty means greatness in appearance, dignity, grandeur, dignity of aspect or manner, and the quality or state of a person who inspires awe or reverence. It's a word that can also refer to beauty and Royal power.

All of these words defined the character, the beauty, and the power of Jesus. All of these definitions describe Jesus as being equal in substance, in power, in glory, and in majesty with God.

Because of who He is and the glory that fills Him, he inspires reverence in us. He fills us with awe and wonder about His greatness and love for us. It is a wonderful thought when we consider that this majestic God would want anything to do with us. It is an even more wonderful thought when we consider that this majestic God, who is, above all, would want to become like us.

How do we wrap our minds around the fact that God would become a man so that we could have a relationship with him? We have nothing in us that is worthy of his attention. Yet He reveals Himself to us so that we can know Him and have a relationship with Him. Once we know Jesus as our personal savior, his majesty fills us. His glory and his love move us to want to want to know him.

Not only is Jesus the substance and the image of the invisible God. **He is also eternal in nature and being.** Jesus did not begin at his birth in Bethlehem. Jesus was not a created being like you and I are. He is eternal. He existed long before anything was ever created. He was there in eternity before the world, and the heavens were formed.

Jesus referred to his eternal nature several times during his ministry on earth. He told the religious leaders **before Abraham existed I am. (John 8:58)** He described himself with the same phrase that God used when he spoke to Moses at the burning bush.

The Lord told Moses that he was to go back to Egypt and lead the children of Israel to the promised land. Moses gave all kinds of excuses as to why he could not do that. Eventually, Moses knew that he had to be obedient to what the Lord asked him to do. He then asked the Lord what his name was. He said that when he went back to Egypt, the people would want to know who sent him. And so, he asked what is your name? It was then the Lord said **I am that I am. (Exodus 3:14)**

Jesus used this same name to describe himself. He was telling those religious leaders that he was there long before Abraham was even born. He was saying His life is not like the life of everyone else. Abraham, like every person on Earth, had a beginning and an end. Jesus was letting the religious leaders know that he had no beginning and he has no end. He was before Abraham. He was in eternity before Abraham was ever born. And being the "I am," he will be in eternity after everyone and everything else is gone.

John 17 describes the prayer that Jesus prayed just before his crucifixion. In that prayer, He speaks about returning to the Father. In verse five, he prays **Now, Father, bring me into the glory we shared before the world began.** It is another of those passages where Jesus speaks about his eternal nature. He was with the Father before the world was created. He was with the Father before the breath of God breathed into dust to create life. Jesus is now saying that he's going to return to the Father. He is looking forward to the glory that awaits him.

The writer of Hebrews speaks about this awaiting glory in chapter 12. **Looking to Jesus, the founder, and perfecter of our faith, who for the joy that was set before him endured the cross, despising the shame, and is seated at the right hand of the throne of God. (Hebrews 12:2 ESV)**

It was this anticipation of returning to glory that gave Jesus the power to go through all of the suffering on the cross. He knew that on the other side of the cross was heaven. He knew that on the other side of the cross was a glory that he once had. Knowing that this awaited him, he was willing to go through all of the torture, pain, and suffering so that you and I could be saved.

Another example of Jesus referring to his eternity is in Revelation 22:13. He told John. **I am the Alpha and Omega, the beginning and the end, the first and the last. (NLT)** The idea here is that he originated everything, and he will see and develop the end of everything. He determined how salvation would take place and how he would bring the completion of this salvation in heaven. He is the one presiding over and controlling everything. He formed the world, and he will wind up its affairs. He is the beginning, the continuance, and the end of all things.

Jesus gave up his majesty to become like us.

Paul speaks to this in the letter to the Philippians 2:6-8. **Let this mind be in you that was in Christ Jesus, who exists in the form of God, did not consider equality as something to be grasped but emptied himself, taking upon himself the form of a servant being made in human likeness. (NLT)**

There is a depth of wonder, amazement, and knowledge in considering all that is said here and all that it means. Look at each individual point.

Jesus was equal to God.

Jesus emptied himself, meaning that he gave up the powers and glory of God, the majesty of heaven, and his authority over angels.

He gave up all of that glory to become a man. There are so many things to consider when we speak of the glory and the majesty of Jesus. Every time the glory of God is referred to in scripture, it is described as being overwhelming, frightening, and beautiful at the same time. It is a glory that is so wonderful that those who find themselves in its presence want to see more. They wanted to see the fullness of that beauty.

Consider for a moment the implications of what Jesus gave up to become a man. Isaiah says that he gave up the beauty of his glory to become an ordinary-looking man.

Isaiah 52:2-3 says He grew up before him like a tender shoot, and like a root out of dry ground. He had no beauty or majesty to attract us to him, nothing in his appearance that we should desire him.

According to Isaiah, Jesus would not have been considered a handsome man. When Isaiah says that he had no beauty to attract anyone to him means that he was not a good-looking man.

Some people might ask, why is that important? What does it matter that he was not good-looking? It matters because of how the world focuses on appearance. Billions of dollars are spent every year on beauty products. Even more money is spent on facial reconstruction, facelifts, tummy tucks, liposuction, and so many other procedures, that are to make us look good.

The fashion industry tells us that what we wear is important because that is the first impression we make on other people. Jesus wanted us to know that he did not want people to follow him because of his appearance. He wanted people to follow him because of his message. He wanted people to follow Him because of who He was. He was the son of God who came to save men from their sins.

Jesus emphasizes that God is much more concerned about what is in the heart and mind rather than what kind of clothes we are wearing or what kind of makeup we have on.

Jesus not only gave up the beauty of his majesty and glory, he also gave up his power. Isaiah 40:12 says **Who else has held the oceans in his hand? Who has measured off the heavens with his fingers? Who else knows the weight of the earth or has weighed the mountains and hills on a scale?**

This is an amazing verse that shows the power, authority, and largeness of God. The point of this verse is to show that our God is larger than his creation. He holds the oceans in his hands. He measures the heavens.

Now consider for a moment who we are in the vastness of these creations. Our planet, Earth, is an insignificant planet in the midst of the universe. One writer stated that there are more stars in the heavens than there are grains of sand on the beaches of the world. Our world is like a molecule in the midst of all we see. Once we travel outside of our Milky Way, earth cannot be seen. It becomes nothing more than a small flickering light.

Jesus, who created the universe, holds all creation together. This one who sat on the throne of creation as Lord gave all of that up to become a human being on an insignificant planet. This is how far Jesus stooped to change our eternity.

I tried to think about what to compare this extreme act to. In a simple example, Jesus coming to earth as a man would be similar to a full-grown man becoming an ant or a bug. Jesus stooped this low to bring us to heaven. Paul says that Jesus becoming a man was for more than just bringing us to heaven. His reason for coming was to give us something that we could not get for ourselves. He came to give us a life full of his presence. He came to was to give us His riches in glory. He came to fill us with himself.

Paul speaks about this in 2 Corinthians 8:9: **You know the generous grace of our Lord Jesus Christ. Though he was rich, yet for your sake, he became poor so that by his poverty, he could make you rich. (NLT)**

This is another one of those passages of scripture that reveals all Jesus gave up in order to become human. When Paul says that Jesus was rich, we do not have the ability to fathom all of his riches. Here is the one who sits on the throne of heaven. It is by his word everything we see and don't see was created.

He gave up all of that glory and riches to come down to earth and live among us. When he was here, he did not have any worldly riches. The New Testament says that Jesus did not have a house to live in. He did not hold some high-paying and popular positions in some large companies. Jesus did none of those. He literally emptied Himself of anything that had material value. Paul says that the reason Jesus gave up all of his riches was because he wanted to make us rich. The riches that Jesus is talking about are not material riches. It is not money in the bank, large amounts of stocks and bonds, or multiple houses. It is not unusual for people to have all of these riches mentioned above and still be impoverished in their lives. It is very possible to have all kinds of material wealth and be utterly empty spiritually.

Jesus teaches us that no matter how much property we own or how much money we have in the bank, we can still be miserable. He came to do something exceptional for our hearts, mind, and emotions. He wants us to be happy and full in our Christian lives. He is talking about making us rich in our spiritual lives.

Matthew 19:16-22 is an example of why Jesus gave up heaven to become like us.

And behold, one came and said to Him.

Good Master, what good thing shall I do that I may have eternal life? And He said to him, why do you call Me good? *There is* none good but one that is, God. But if you want to enter into life, keep the commandments. He said to Him, Which? Jesus said, you shall not murder, you shall not commit adultery, you shall not steal, you shall not bear false witness, honor your father and mother, and you shall love your neighbor as yourself.

The young man said to Him, I have kept all these things from my youth up; what do I lack yet? Jesus said to him If you want to be perfect, go, sell what you have and give to *the* poor, and you shall have treasure in Heaven. And come, follow Me. But when the young man heard that saying, he went away sorrowful, for he had great possessions. Then Jesus said to His disciples, Truly I say to you that a rich man will with great difficulty enter into the kingdom of Heaven.

Here is the story of a very wealthy young man. He is described as a ruler, meaning that he had some kind of position or authority because of his wealth. Even though he had everything he wanted materially, he still felt that something was missing in his life. He still was not satisfied.

So, he came to Jesus, knowing in his heart that something was missing in his life. Jesus told him that the reason he was not satisfied was because he had his priorities and focus in the wrong place. His priority was his wealth. Even though He was concerned about his spiritual condition, he was more focused on his material wealth. How do we know this? We know this from his response when Jesus told him to sell his riches and then follow Him. When Jesus told the young man what to do, he refused. He could not give up all of his material possessions. He wanted to keep his riches and just add spiritual security to his life.

He did not understand that if he gave everything away, all that Jesus would give him would be more than enough to fill his life. Jesus wanted to fill him up with spiritual fruit and spiritual gifts. He wanted this young man to experience the reality that when his life is filled with spiritual gifts and riches, then he would experience fulfillment he did not think was even possible. Sadly, he walked away from what Jesus offered.

The eternal glory of Jesus was witnessed after his resurrection.

Earlier, we spoke about the prayer Jesus prayed in John 17. It was in that prayer that he asked the Father to return Him to the glory He once had. At the time of this prayer, Jesus was already feeling the weight of sin that was being laid on Him. He was already feeling the agony of the cross.

After that prayer and after spending agonizing moments in the Garden of Gethsemane, Jesus was crucified. Afterward, he was buried in a borrowed tomb. Gloriously, three days later, the stone in front of the tomb was rolled away, and Jesus arose. When Jesus came out of that grave, he came out with a glorified, eternal body.

This body was no longer limited to time and space. Jesus could appear and disappear at will. He could walk with some of his disciples for miles, talking to them and teaching them without them ever knowing who he was. He could determine when to reveal Himself to his followers.

However, even after the resurrection from the grave, Jesus continued to veil or hide the fullness of his glory. At other times, Jesus revealed the fullness of his eternal glory. Eventually, the time came for Jesus to return to His Father. It came time for the Father to answer the prayer Jesus prayed in John 17.

Jesus' eternal glory was witnessed by his ascension into heaven.

Acts 1:9 records the moment that Jesus left this world and ascended back to the Father.

And when he had spoken these things, while they beheld, he was taken up, and a cloud received him out of their sight. (KJV)

The ascension of Jesus was important for the disciples to witness. Even as Jesus was getting ready to leave, the disciples were still thinking of the Kingdom of God as something that was going to happen on earth. Before he ascended, his disciples wanted to know when the kingdom was going to come. They were still thinking of an earthly kingdom.

The ascension was a reminder to them that His kingdom was not of this world. His kingdom was heavenly and spiritual. They had yet to learn this lesson.

Since He ascended into heaven, the scriptures give accounts of visions of the fullness of the glory of God.

Stephen, the first martyr, saw the eternal glory of Jesus before he was stoned.

Stephen, the first believer to be martyred because of his faith, was able to see into heaven and the fullness of the glory of God. Stephen knew he was about to die, and in that moment, God gave him a vision of Jesus on his heavenly throne.

But he, being full of the Holy Ghost, looked up steadfastly into heaven and saw the glory of God, and Jesus standing on the right hand of God,

And said, Behold, I see the heavens opened, and the Son of man standing on the right hand of God. Then they cried out with a loud voice, and stopped their ears, and ran upon him with one accord, And cast him out of the city, and stoned him: and the witnesses laid down their clothes at a young man's feet, whose name was Saul. (Acts 7:55-58). (KJV)

Stephen was put on trial for his faith and testimony concerning Jesus. When he was on trial, he was given the opportunity to defend himself for his testimony and his preaching about Jesus. Instead of defending himself, he gives the history of Israel and how it failed as a nation. He speaks of their rebellion against God all through their history. He then accuses them of rejecting the Son of God and crucifying Him. This accusation drove the religious leaders into a rage. The Bible says they took Stephen and stoned him to death. Just before he died, he looked up and was able to see the throne of God in heaven. He said **I see the glory of God and Jesus standing next to the throne of God.** God let Stephen His glory. Most of all, He let Stephen see Jesus in his glory.

The apostle John gave descriptive pictures of the glory of Jesus.

In Revelation 1, John has a vision of the glorified Christ.

I, John, *who* also *am* **your brother and companion in the affliction and in the kingdom and patience of Jesus Christ, was on the island that is called Patmos for the Word of God and for the testimony of Jesus Christ. I came to be in** *the* **Spirit in the Lord's Day and heard behind me a great voice, as of a trumpet, saying, I am the Alpha and Omega, the First and the Last. Also, what you see, write in a book and send** *it* **to the seven churches which are in Asia: to Ephesus, and to Smyrna, and to Pergamos, and to Thyatira, and to Sardis, and to Philadelphia, and to Laodicea And I turned to see the voice that spoke with me.**

And having turned, I saw seven golden lampstands. And in the midst of the seven lampstands, I saw One like the Son of man, clothed with a garment down to the feet and tied around the breast with a golden band. His head and hair *were* **white like wool, as white as snow. And His eyes** *were* **like a flame of fire. And His feet were like burnished brass having been fired in a furnace. And His voice was like the sound of many waters. And He had seven stars in His right hand, and out of His mouth went a sharp two-edged sword. And His face** *was* **like the sun shining in its strength. And when I saw Him, I fell at His feet as dead. And He laid His right hand upon me, saying to me, Do not fear, I am the First and the Last, and the Living One, and I became dead, and behold, I am alive forever and ever, Amen. And I have the keys of hell and of death. (Revelation 1:9-20)**

The glory of Jesus referred to in this passage is the same glory revealed by God throughout the scripture. It is a glory that is overwhelming. Men faint when they find themselves in the presence of this glory. God told Moses that **No one can see my glory and**

live. It is this glory that Jesus returned to when he ascended back into heaven.

We began this chapter by speaking about the eternal glory of Jesus. He did not begin his life in Bethlehem. He has always been. It is a glorious thought when we consider this eternal God wants us to be with Him. It is even more wonderful that this glorious God wants to share His glory with us. He wants us to experience the joy and wonder of being in his presence forever. It is difficult to imagine that this eternal glory has been given to us. The glorious Spirit of Jesus lives in us, empowers us and is making us into his image. Those who are believers in Jesus will share this glory forever.

THE PURPOSE OF SCRIPTURE: TO REVEAL HIS GLORY

Throughout this study, we are going to be seeing all of the ways the glory of Jesus was manifested. We would know very little of the glory of Jesus or his character if it had not been revealed to us. God is Spirit. He does not have a body like we have. He is invisible to the human eye. The only way that we can see anything of the glory of God is if He does something that allows us to see Him,

The Old Testament is full of examples where the Lord revealed Himself in a visible way to his people. In Genesis, the Lord appeared to Abraham as a man. He visited Abraham and spent the day talking and entering into a covenant with Him.

He appeared to Moses as a burning bush that would not burn up.

He appeared to the children of Israel as a cloud that would lead them through the day and a pillar of fire that led them at night.

He also appeared to Israel as smoke or clouds on the mountain. These clouds veiled his glory but the people knew He was present with the thunder and the earthquake on the mountain.

He appeared to Israel when the tabernacle was finished. The Bible says that the glory of the Lord descended on the tabernacle, indicating that. God was present with them every day.

He appeared to Joshua as he prepared to enter into battle. When Joshua saw the Lord, he asked, **"Are you with us or against us."** The Lord revealed who He was, and Joshua worshipped Him.

These are just a few examples of how Jesus revealed Himself to men and women who did not have the ability to see Him unless He made Himself visible.

How, then, does He reveal Himself to us?

It has been generations since the Lord made these visible appearances to His people. There have been few instances in the New Testament where He revealed Himself visible. We already mentioned Stephen who the Lord allowed to see into heaven and saw Jesus.

Paul had an experience where he says he was caught up in the third heaven. In that experience, he said that he saw things that were difficult to describe. He inferred that he did not have an adequate vocabulary to describe what he saw in heaven.

John, the apostle, had the final vision of the risen Lord when Jesus appeared to him on the island of Patmos. John was imprisoned there, and Jesus revealed Himself to John and gave directions for writing the book of Revelation.

So then, how do we see Him? How does He reveal Himself to us today? He does it through His word, the Bible. The Bible was given so we might know about Jesus, His person, His glory, His power, His death, burial, and resurrection, and the new life he promises. If, then, we are going to learn about Jesus and grasp who He is and what He has done and is doing, we have to read, study, and meditate on the word of God. The Word was given to us so everything about Jesus could be revealed to us.

Chapter 6
The Glory of His Name; God With Us

MATTHEW 1:23

This took place to fulfill what the Lord had said through the prophet: Behold, the virgin will be with child and will give birth to a son, and they will call Him Immanuel," which means "God with us."

The Bible gives many names concerning Jesus. Isaiah described him as being **the Wonderful Counselor, the Mighty God, the Prince of Peace**. (Is 9:6). All of these names have special significance to us. When we are hurting and need direction in our lives, He is that counselor who knows what to say and how to lead us. When we feel that we are weak and don't have the strength to face all of the trials and obstacles in our lives, he is **the mighty God.** When it seems that things rage against us and we are overwhelmed by all of the problems and trials that we face, he is the **Prince of Peace.** All of these names are special to us and have wonderful meanings through all of the times of our lives.

In this passage, we are given another name of Jesus. He is called **Emmanuel, God with us.** It is this name that describes his glorious presence in us.

A name of humiliation

God with us means that *he became like us.* The God of the universe, the creator of all things, became like that which he created. This is an act of humiliation that you and I cannot begin to understand.

It would have been amazing if God had stooped to become some kind of angelic being. It would have been humiliation enough for him to become a seraphim or a cherubim and then communicate with us.

God went much further down the chain of creation than an angel. He became a man. He stooped down and wrapped himself up in human flesh and became one of us. **He became the weakest of all the creations he made.**

When God became a man, he took upon himself all of those things that were a complete contradiction to him. He was God. As God, he could never be hungry. He could never be thirsty. He could never experience any pain and suffering. When he became a man, he experienced all of those things. He experienced everything that you and I experienced in our lives.

He grew hungry. He grew tired and needed rest. He grieved over the behavior of his friends. He was wounded by the rejection of his own people. God experienced, physically, emotionally, and mentally, all of the things that you and I experience.

This is an event that is too wonderful and too deep to explore. God joined with us. He experienced union with us for one purpose. He was not on some kind of experimental mission. He was not doing research. He became like us so that he might save us from our sins and give us everlasting life.

One preacher said that God experienced the grosser part of his creation so he could deliver us from our sins and give us a home in heaven. It would be a wonder that God would become like a race of people who never sinned. But it is more wonderful that God became like a sinful man. He became like the people who sinned against him. He became like those who broke his law and rebelled against his will. He became like us.

The miraculous revelation of the name.

The great miracle of the incarnation was that God could wrap himself up in the flesh so that men and women could touch him and be in his presence. Because he wrapped himself up in human flesh, men and women could talk with him, look upon him, and see him. They could be in his presence and touch him and handle him. This was a miracle in itself.

We can understand something of this being a miracle when we see something of the overwhelming overpowering glory of God. Every time we see something of the glory of God mentioned in the

Bible, we find that men and women could not look upon it. They could not stand in the presence of the glory of God.

The Lord could not be approached when he appeared on the mountain with Moses.

Exodus 19: 9, 16-21

9 The LORD said to Moses, "Behold, I will come to you in a dense cloud so that the people will hear when I speak with you, and they will always put their trust in you."

And Moses relayed to the LORD what the people had said.

10 Then the LORD said to Moses, "Go to the people and consecrate them today and tomorrow. They must wash their clothes 11 and be prepared by the third day, for on the third day, the LORD will come down on Mount Sinai in the sight of all the people.

12 And you are to set up a boundary for the people around the mountain and tell them, 'Be careful not to go up on the mountain or touch its base. Whoever touches the mountain shall surely be put to death. 13 No hand shall touch him, but he shall surely be stoned or shot with arrows—whether man or beast, he must not live.'

Joshua could not stand in the presence of the Lord when he appeared to him as the captain of the army of the Lord.

(Joshua 5:13-15)

13 Now when Joshua was near Jericho, he looked up and saw a man standing in front of him with a drawn sword in His hand. Joshua approached Him and asked, "Are You for us or for our enemies?"

14"Neither," He replied. "I have now come as Commander of the LORD's army."

Then Joshua fell face down in reverence and asked Him, "What does my Lord have to say to His servant?"

15 The Commander of the LORD's army replied, "Take off your sandals, for the place where you are standing is holy."

And Joshua did so.

There are many other passages of scripture that we could use to show how the presence of the Lord was so overwhelming and powerful that the people could not stand or be in the midst of that presence.

But when God became flesh, men and women could approach him. Little children could sit in his lap. Women could anoint his head and feet with perfume. This one who had mountains tremble at his presence was now touchable and approachable.

His coming in the flesh revealed the desire of his heart. He wants us to be able to approach him. He wants us to be able to come to him. He does not want to be distant from us. He wants to have fellowship with us.

Before he became flesh, we could not do anything of those things. His glory was so overpowering to our sinfulness that we would have died in his presence. But when he became flesh, there was the hiding of that overwhelming glory. There was the veiling of the awesome, glorious majesty of his character.

The fact that he was able to do this was the miracle of creation. We know how frail and weak these bodies are. The apostle Paul called our bodies vessels of clay. But God miraculously hid his glory inside a human body so he could fellowship with us. This is the miracle of Christmas.

GOD WITH US IS A PLEDGE OF OUR DELIVERANCE.

We are a fallen people. We have sinned against Almighty God. We are not deserving of anything good that he gives to us, especially his presence. Before God came, we were under the bondage and the penalty of sin. But now we are free because God is with us. We are no longer in bondage because God is with us.

Those things which held us slaves to sin can no longer hold us because God is with us. Jesus coming down from heaven, taking upon himself our nature, taking up our cause and our battles is assurance that we will experience victory over our eternal enemy of sin and death. Jesus coming down and wrapping himself up in the flesh is our guarantee that we shall be set from and have eternal life.

If any other heavenly creature came down and fought for us we might have our doubts about the assurance of our salvation. But it was not some heavenly powerful creature, it was God himself who came down with us to be for us and to deliver us.

It was God with us who came down to be for us and deliver us.

It was God with us who came to set us free for eternity, free to have a relationship with him.

Look at all the implications for us when Jesus became like us.

1. To be with us means to be close to us.

The Greek word <u>with</u> means much more than just being in the company of someone. It is a word that means to be together with, to share with. It is a word that means a firm bond and a close fellowship. It means to be in close association with someone.

God with us means that we have a unique eternal bond with him that he initiated. We did not seek to be with him because of the sinful nature of our lives, but he sought to be with us. He initiated the plan and carried out the plan to put him with us.

2. He is with us in all the journeys of our lives.

We do not have any place we can go or have any experience where He is not there.

Read Psalm 139: 7-11

<u>7</u> Where can I go to escape Your Spirit?

Where can I flee from your presence

<u>8</u> If I ascend to the heavens, You are there;

if I make my bed in Sheol, You are there.

<u>9</u> If I rise on the wings of the dawn,

if I settle by the farthest sea,

<u>10</u> even there, Your hand will guide me;

Your right hand will hold me fast.

11If I say, "Surely the darkness will hide me,

and the light become night around me"—

12even the darkness is not dark to You,

but the night shines like the day,

for darkness is as light to You. (NKJV)

He is there at the birth of our children and through the experiences of raising them.

At the same time, he is with Christian young people who live with parents who do not live the Christian life or have the Christian values they believe in. God is with them in strengthening them during this growing up time.

He is there when we begin our family.

He is there at our wedding.

He is there on our job.

He is there when we get that promotion or when we lose that job.

He is there when we lose someone in death.

He is with us in the battles and trials we go through.

He is there in the class room with us.

He is there in our old age when things begin to slip away.

He is there when we fail or when we are alone.

He is there when we face death.

Most of us remember the tragic event that happened on the Texas A&M campus with the collapse of the setup for a bonfire. Twelve young people died in that accident. The twelve who died were truly remarkable kids. They were scholars, students, and active in Boy Scouts, 4-H, and Church groups. They were leaders. If you had to choose a dozen students to represent the best of Texas A&M, you probably wouldn't do much better than these.

My Daughter and son-in-law were at A&M when this happened. After this tragedy, I learned about a young man, Timothy Doran Kerlee Jr. He was the twelfth student to die. When the stack collapsed, his pelvis was crushed, his arm was broken, and his internal organs were scrambled like an omelet. He was one of those who was trapped but would not allow rescue workers to help him until they got to all of the other students who were below him. He was actually directing the rescue efforts of the other students who were trapped. He kept telling them that he was O.K., And he directed the rescuers to at least five other students before he allowed them to take him down from the stack.

He was taken into the emergency room, where they took X-rays and imaging and found that his organs were so badly damaged that they couldn't identify much of what they saw. They closed him up, wrapped him in a sheet to hold him together, and placed him on life support. He lived long enough to see and speak to his parents. He was aware that he was dying and asked not to be placed on life support. When his parents asked him why he wanted to, he asked them why he should fight for a few more days of life when he could be in heaven with Jesus in a few moments. He knew that the Lord was with him. There was no fear in him, no hesitation about what he wanted to do. Emmanuel: God with us was there with this young man at the time of his death. Timothy Kerlee knew that and felt confident and hopeful at the end of his life. (A Chance to say goodby: Hope for Grieving Parents; written by Janice Kerlee, January 4, 2004)

3. He is with us in blessed communication

Once we enter into a relationship with him, he continues to communicate his will to us.

He communicates his pleasure, his direction for our lives, and his love. One of the things that we try to tell married couples and those going through pre-marital counseling is that one of the most important features of their marriage is how they communicate with one another. We tell them that communication is one of those keys that builds intimacy, strength and endurance in a marriage or in any other relationship.

God knows the value and the importance of communication. And he communicates with us continually. He wants us to know about himself, his will, and his direction for our lives. He communicates with us through his word. He communicates through prayer, and he communicates through his moving and working in our lives.

In all of the communication of God, there is one message that stands out. God wants the best for us. God says in his word. **"All things work out for good for those who love the Lord and who are called according to his purpose. (Romans 8:28 KJV)**

3. He is with us in our blessed restoration.

In an area near downtown Lake Charles, where I lived, there is an area known as the historical district. In that area are some of the older homes in the city. It is really an amazing thing to see what many people are doing to those homes. They move into them and restore them. They refurbish them to where they look like they did many years ago. They restore them to beauty and value.

This is what God is doing in our lives. He is renewing us to be what we were once created to be. When God created Adam and Eve, he created them in perfection and beauty. But they sinned, and they lost the beauty and perfection of their lives. They became sinners, separated from God. God knew all of this was going to happen. So when Adam and Eve sinned, God was not caught off guard. He already determined what he would do. He determined this before he ever created the world.

This is why Jesus was born. He came so that through his death on the cross, we could be restored to the image of God. Colossians 3:1-10 says

<u>1</u> Therefore, since you have been raised with Christ, strive for the things above, where Christ is seated at the right hand of God.

<u>2</u> Set your mind on things above, not on earthly things.

<u>3</u> For you died, and your life is now hidden with Christ in God.

<u>4</u> When Christ, who is your life, appears, then you also will appear with Him in glory.

<u>5</u> Put to death, therefore, the components of your earthly nature: sexual immorality, impurity, lust, evil desires, and greed, which is idolatry.

<u>6</u> Because of these, the wrath of God is coming on the sons of disobedience.

<u>7</u> When you lived among them, you also used to walk in these ways.

<u>8</u> But now you must put aside all such things as these: anger, rage, malice, slander, and filthy language from your lips.

<u>9</u> Do not lie to one another since you have taken off the old self with its practices,

<u>10</u> and have put on the new self, which is being renewed in knowledge in the image of its Creator. (NIV)

Notice the phrase **Who is being renewed in knowledge and the image of its creator."** the renewal or the restoration of knowledge is not the knowledge of everything, but it is the knowledge of God. It is that ability and that privilege of knowing him.

Before the fall, Adam and Eve knew God. They walked with God in the garden. They had fellowship with him. After the fall, they no longer had that personal fellowship with God. They were kicked out of the visible, intimate experience with God. They were far away because of sin. God already had a plan in place to restore their relationship with him. That plan involved a cross with his son on it.

And when Jesus came, he closed the gap between us and him. Now, those who trusted Jesus as their personal savior are being renewed in their knowledge of him. We can know more about him now because of our relationship with him.

Not only are we being renewed in our knowledge of him, **but we are also being renewed in the image of the Creator.** This means that we are becoming more and more like Jesus in our lives. It means that we are growing in righteousness, grace, love, peace, and other God-like qualities. God is in the midst of the greatest restoration project the world has ever known, he is restoring us to be like himself.

My wife and I have a favorite show on TV that features two men who go into an impoverished community to buy homes that are in terrible condition. They then restore those homes. The people of the community express gratitude for what these men are doing. They are doing more than just restoring a house. They are helping restore a community. Those restoration projects are nothing compared to the restoration that God is doing in our lives. He is not making us better. He is not improving on what we are. He is making everything new. We are a new creation being renewed into the image of Christ.

But this is not the way you came to know Christ. Surely you heard of Him and were taught in Him—in keeping with the truth that is in Jesus to put off your former way of life, your old self, which is being corrupted by its deceitful desires, To be renewed in the spirit of your minds; And to put on the new self, created to be like God in true righteousness and holiness. (Ephesians 4:20-24, NKJV)

Paul states here that the restoration that is taking place in us is the creation of a new attitude, a new self. This new self is created to be like Christ in righteousness and holiness. And the one who is with us is the one who is doing this restoration. Emmanuel, God with us is restoring our lives to be like him. We can now see that this name is the most precious name that Jesus could have in regard to us. God is with us. When we go out into a hostile world, God is with us. When times are tough or when they are good, God is with us. Let us celebrate that God loves us so much that he wants to be with us. Let us celebrate one of the great miracles of all eternity, **Emmanuel: God with us.**

This is really a remarkable passage of scripture. God is with us. Each one of us who has a personal relationship with Jesus has this unique, intimate relationship with him. He is not just with us, but he is in us. He is not with us just to be an observer of our life. No, he is with us to be the guide and the director of our life. He is with us to help us through our daily affairs.

I know that some people think that there are things in our lives that God is not interested in. They think that God does not concern himself with the small details of our life. If we think that, then we need to correct that thinking. We need to understand that there is not a part of our life that the Lord is not interested in. He is aware of all the details of our life. He knows what you are going through today. He knows if you had a bad week or faced serious problems. He knows if you were persecuted or mocked because of your faith.

He cares about what we experience and what we do. Do not think that things in your life are not interesting to the Lord. He is passionate about everything in our life. He wants to fill our lives with his presence, his knowledge, his power, and his grace. When we sin, he is with us to forgive us. When we fall, he is with us to pick us up. When we are mocked, he is with us to tell us the truth about who we are. He is with each of us in a very special way. If we can remember that, it helps us get through whatever experiences we face. He wants to be with you in a very special way. He wants to be with you in a permanent, indwelling relationship. The only way that can happen is by trusting and believing in Jesus.

Chapter 7
A Glorious Song

LUKE 1:46-56

When we experience something wonderful in our lives, we just want to express our joy over it to the best of our ability. When a new baby is born in the family, everyone is excited and ready to tell anyone who will listen about this birth. When you are job hunting and the employer calls to say you've been selected, it's a joy worth sharing. And then, when the doctor says that he can't find any trace of cancer, we just want to share that with someone. We want to tell good news. We want to express our feelings of joy.

This is what this passage of scripture is about. Mary is pregnant with the son of God. She had a visit from an angel who told her of great things that were going to happen. In the early stages of her pregnancy, she goes and visits her cousin, Elizabeth. When she arrives, Elizabeth expresses great joy and excitement. The Bible says that even the baby she is carrying jumps for joy. This whole event is so exciting that it seems there are no words to describe how they are feeling.

Mary, under the inspiration of the Holy Spirit, sings this song. It is a song that expresses the feelings in her heart and what she feels is a need to glorify the Lord. And that is how she begins. **My soul magnifies the Lord.** In another translation, she says, **my heart praises the Lord.** In the Living Bible says, **Oh how I praise the Lord.**

She praises the Lord because he noticed her.

Mary realized that in the eyes of the world, she was a nobody. She knows that she is unknown, insignificant, and of little value and importance to the world. God saw her in that condition and changed her life. Because of what God did for her and how He used her, she became the most highly regarded woman in the world. She describes herself as a **lowly servant.** Some believe that the language she uses to describe herself in this passage indicates that she is the least important in her own family; maybe the youngest daughter.

This lowly position did not prevent God from using her/. When we consider the wording of this passage in the context of Mary and reflect on our own lives, we too can also rejoice because God has noticed us. We were not just in a lowly state,We were lost in sin. We were separated from God and on our way to hell, but God noticed us. He saw us in this condition, and he changed us. He gave us life. He gave us a home in heaven. He paid the price for our sins. We, too, can say, **My soul does magnify the Lord.**

Rom 5:8

8 But God demonstrates His own love toward us in that while we were still sinners, Christ died for us.

1 Peter 3:18

For Christ also suffered once for sins, the just for the unjust, that He might bring us to God, being put to death in the flesh but made alive by the Spirit,

These passages should not just bring a sense of joy to each one of us but also give hope to anyone who feels that they are not worthy of the blessings of God. I met many people in my life who feel that they are not worthy of God's salvation. They feel that they have done too many things wrong for God to love them and do anything about their spiritual condition. Mary rejoices that God noticed her in the lowly, insignificant position she was in.

This shows us that God notices us in the poor spiritual condition we are in. Indeed, we are not worthy of the love and the forgiveness of God. It is true that we are not worthy of his salvation. It is true that we do not deserve his love. But our worthiness is not what determines God's love for us. He loves us no matter what. He wants to save us from our sins no matter what we have done.

The apostle Paul declared that he was the worst sinner who ever lived. He described himself as the **chief of sinners.** Paul testifies that God loved and saved the chief of sinners. If he can do that, he can save anyone seeking salvation from him. So don't ever think you are out of the reach of God. He sent Jesus to reach you in the worst of spiritual conditions.

God took an insignificant young lady and made her the most notable woman in the world. He chose someone who seemed to have no worth and made her the mother of Jesus. She said that every generation shall call her blessed. It is this very thing that Jesus desires to do with every person who believes him. He wants to give them not just life, but he wants to bless them with abundant life.

John 10:10

10 The thief does not come except to steal, and to kill, and to destroy. I have come that they may have life, and that they may have it more abundantly.

James 4:10

Humble yourselves in the sight of the Lord, and he shall lift you up."

She praises God because of his glorious character:

She praises him for his great, miraculous act. For he who is mighty has done great things for me. She is thinking about the incarnation here. She is thinking about this virgin conception. She has never had physical relations with anyone, and now she finds that she is pregnant because of the work of the Holy Spirit. What has happened to her has never happened before and has never happened since. What has happened to her could only come about because of the power of God.

Another great demonstration of the power of God is seen in the fact that the glory of God was concealed in a human being. In the Old Testament, the Shekinah glory of God was described as so overwhelming that people could not stand in the presence of God. When the glory of God entered the Tabernacle, men and women had to get out. When the glory of God entered the temple, no one could enter the temple. When the glory of God appeared on a mountain, the people were told not to come near the mountain or to touch the mountain. But now, this glory is wrapped up in the human flesh of a baby. This is the greatest miracle of all.

She praises him for his mercy. She says that his mercy is on them that fear him. The word that she uses for fear here is not a cringing fear. It is not the fear of being hurt or abused. The fear that

Mary is describing here is a reverent fear. It is the fear of hurting or wounding the one we love. It is the fear of offending God or dishonoring him. Mary says that those who have this fear are men and women who have experienced the mercy of God.

We, like Mary, can praise the Lord for his mercy. It was because of his mercy that we have new life. It was because of his mercy that Jesus went to the cross. It was because of his mercy that he gave forgiveness. It was because of his mercy that he provided salvation for those who were lost. We can praise him for his mercy.

"It is because of the LORD's mercies that we are not consumed; his compassions do not fail. They are new every morning: great is your faithfulness" (Lament. 3:22-23**).**

Mic 7:18-20

18 Where is another God like you, who pardons the sins of the survivors among his people? You cannot stay angry with your people forever because you delight in showing mercy. 19 Once again, you will have compassion on us. You will trample our sins under your feet and throw them into the depths of the ocean! 20 You will show us your faithfulness and unfailing love as you promised with an oath to our ancestors Abraham and Jacob long ago.

She praises him for his strength. She says that God has shown strength with his arm. One commentary says that this means that *He has gained the victory.* When we think about the reason that Jesus came, we rejoice because he did gain the victory. He gained the victory over sin when he died on the cross. He gained the victory over death when he rose again on the third day. And he gained the victory over hell because the Bible says that he now has the keys to death and hell. In other words, he has control over these things.

We then can rejoice because he gained the victory over our lives. He was victorious over our own rebellious nature. He was victorious over our unbelief. He was victorious over the spiritual death in our lives and has given us eternal life.

This God of strength and power now lives in believers. He has the power to answer our prayers. He has the power to heal us of our diseases. He has the power to save us from sin and to keep us saved. We can rejoice that he has this kind of power. We can rejoice in this power because it is the power of God that provides for all our needs. It is this power in us that helps us live the way God wants us to live.

She praises the Lord for his spiritual nourishment. He satisfied the hungry with good things. Oh, think of the good things the Lord has given us to eat. Think of those wonderful things the Lord has done to fill us up so that we want nothing but him.

He fills us up with himself:

Ps 34:8-10

8 Oh, taste and see that the LORD is good;

Blessed is the man who trusts in Him!

9 Oh, fear the LORD, you His saints!

There is no want to those who fear Him.

10 The young lions lack and suffer hunger;

But those who seek the LORD shall not lack any good thing.

John 6:35

35 And Jesus said to them, "I am the bread of life. He who comes to Me shall never hunger, and he who believes in Me shall never thirst.

He fills us up with his word

Ps 119:103

103 How sweet are Your words to my taste,

Sweeter than honey to my mouth!

He fills us up with his faithfulness.

Ps 37:3

3 Trust in the LORD, and do good;

Dwell in the land, and feed on His faithfulness.

She praises the Lord for keeping His promise to Israel.

Verse 55 says, the Lord made this promise to Abraham..(CEV). She says that God remembered the promise that he made to Abraham that a great nation would come from him. This nation would number like the stars in heaven and the sand on the sea. He remembered the promise that he made to Moses that a Messiah would come to Israel. He remembered the promise He made to Isaiah that A WONDERFUL COUNSELOR AND A MIGHTY GOD WOULD BE BORN. HE PROMISED THAT THE PRINCE OF PEACE WOULD BE BORN. God was now fulfilling that promise through Mary. God was fulfilling this promise at a time when the people of Israel desperately needed God's mercy and God's deliverance. They were enslaved by Rome. Their religion was stale and oppressive. They were praying and looking forward to the coming of the Messiah. Now He was here.

Paul reminds us that God is faithful to keep His promises in Gal 3:15-18

15 Dear brothers and sisters, here's an example from everyday life. Just as no one can set aside or amend an irrevocable agreement, so it is in this case. 16 God gave the promise to Abraham and his child. And notice that it doesn't say the promise was to his children as if it meant many descendants. But the promise was to his child--and that, of course, means Christ. 17 This is what I am trying to say: The agreement God made with Abraham could not be canceled 430 years later when God gave the law to Moses. God would be breaking his promise. 18 For if the inheritance could be received only by keeping the law, then it would not be the result of accepting God's promise. But God gave it to Abraham as a promise.

Even though this promise was made hundreds of years before, God did not forget his promise. Just as He did not forget His promises He made to Israel, He does not forget the promises He make to us. He promised to give everlasting life to those who believe in Jesus. He promised that this everlasting life He gave would never be taken away from us. It is eternal life. He promised to fill us with the presence of the Holy Spirit. He promised to answer our prayers. He promised to make a home in heaven for us. Most of all He promised to never leave us or forsake us. You and I can rejoice that God does not forget the promises he makes to us. He is faithful to keep His promises even when we do not keep the promises we make to Him.

There are many times I make promises to God that I do not keep. There are times that I make commitments that I do not keep. There are times when I forget the things I need to do, but God never forgets the promises He makes to me. There are hundreds of promises that God has made to me in the Bible. You and I can spend hours looking through the word of God to see the promises that were made, and we can rejoice that God never forgets one of them.

Let us be like Mary and rejoice in God, our Savior, for all that he is and all the wonderful things he has done.

Chapter 8
The Glory of His Birth

And the angel said unto them, Fear not: for, behold, I bring you good tidings of great joy, which shall be to all people. For unto you is born this day in the city of David a Savior, which is Christ the Lord. And this shall be a sign unto you; Ye shall find the babe wrapped in swaddling clothes, lying in a manger."—Luke 2:10-12.

The people who were in Bethlehem on the night of Jesus' birth were unaware they were living in the greatest historical moment of all time. The crowds of people who were there were concerned about housing, shelter, food, paying their taxes, and going home. They were unaware that God was acting in a way that was going to change the world.

Sadly, this is still the case. Every Christmas season, families get caught up in gift buying, Black Friday sales, Christmas decorations, and trees. Every year, it seems that the planning for Christmas starts earlier and earliest, but the planning has nothing to do with Jesus; it has to do with buying and selling. People today have the same problem as the people of Bethlehem that first Christmas. They missed out on the **news of great joy.**

The small town of Bethlehem was overrun with families who arrived to follow the decree of Caesar to be registered. Everyone had to return to their hometown to fulfill this tax registration. God used this decree by Caesar to accomplish and fulfill what was said in the Old Testament.

Micah 5:2 says **But you, O Bethlehem Ephrathah, who are too little to be among the clans of Judah, from you shall come forth for me one who is to be ruler in Israel, whose coming forth is from of old, from ancient days.**

Micah prophesies that the savior and the ruler of Israel is going to be born in Bethlehem. God either used the circumstances created by Caesar or compelled Caesar to make this decree so Jesus could be born in Bethlehem. The birth of Jesus was the fulfillment of Old Testament prophecy. Jesus said He came to fulfill the Law. His birth was the beginning of that fulfillment.

This place of his birth was not chosen by accident. It was determined that His son would be born in Bethlehem. The name Bethlehem means "House of Bread." It is an appropriate place for the one who called Himself the bread of Life.

It is also good to notice how short the account of Jesus' birth is presented in Luke. He only uses seven verses to describe the greatest event in history that was God becoming a man. In just a few descriptive phrases, Luke says Jesus was born. He gives little details of that birth experience.

One commentator suggests that the brevity of the account of Jesus' birth is due to its perceived ordinariness. What do I mean by that? It means that Jesus was born just like any other child was born. He was delivered in the same way that all other children are birthed.

The miracle of how he was conceived

The emphasis of the birth of Jesus is not so much on the actual birth but on the conception itself. Jesus was conceived in a supernatural way. He was conceived by the work of the Holy Spirit in the life of Mary. The angel that spoke to Mary told her that **the Holy Spirit will come upon you and the power of the Most High will overshadow you; therefore, the child to be born will be called holy—the Son of God. (Luke 1:35).** It was not the birth that was miraculous and supernatural; it was how he was conceived.

Jesus was conceived by the **overshadowing of the Holy Spirit.** This same thought is presented in the book of Genesis, where it describes the creation of the world. **In the beginning, God created the heavens and the earth. The earth was without form and void, and darkness was over the face of the deep. And the Spirit of God was hovering over the face of the waters. (Genesis 1:1-2).** The word used for hovering can also be translated as "brooding" or "overshadowing." When the Holy Spirit hovered over the darkness and the void in the beginning, a new creation was formed. It was a new heaven and earth created through the power of this hovering Spirit.

As we examine the conception of Jesus, the Bible uses the same kind of terminology. The Spirit hovered over Mary. Then, through His creative power, she conceived the Son of God.

I want to call your attention to another hovering activity of the Holy Spirit. It is found in the New Birth Experience. Just as the Holy Spirit created heaven and earth in the beginning and just as he overshadowed Mary to create the human life of Jesus, this same Holy Spirit is also responsible for the creation of the new life that is in us.

Jesus told Nicodemus that a person could not enter into heaven unless he was born again. Nicodemus did not understand the concept, and Jesus told him.

Truly, truly, I say to you, unless one is born of water and the Spirit, he cannot enter the kingdom of God. That which is born of the flesh is flesh, and that which is born of the Spirit is spirit. Do not marvel that I said to you, 'You must be born again.' The wind blows where it wishes, and you hear its sound, but you do not know where it comes from or where it goes. So, it is with everyone who is born of the Spirit." (John 3:5-8)

Jesus made it very clear that there cannot be a spiritual new birth without the working and the creative power of the Holy Spirit. We are what we are as believers not because of anything we have done, but everything God has done to us and for us. The Holy Spirit overshadowed us and provided a New Birth in us. He made us a **new creation.** We are not the same since he moved in our hearts. We are new. Once, we were sinners doomed for an eternity of separation from God; now, we are the Children of God on our way to spend eternity with Him.

Even though the birth of Jesus was ordinary in a sense, it was like all other children. However, The events surrounding his birth were far from ordinary. His coming into the world was a miracle in so many ways. God became a man. More than that, God stopped down to become a baby. That is a remarkable thought. It reveals the depth Jesus stooped so we could have eternal life.

Luke gives historical details of the birth of Jesus.

He was born in poverty. If Joseph had any money, he could have probably gotten a room, but he had none. Jesus left the riches of heaven and became part of a family that had to struggle to survive in the economic world. Joseph was a carpenter, so Jesus learned the carpenter's trade as He grew up. The word carpenter does not describe someone who would be considered a big contractor, doing large jobs and hiring others to work for him. The carpenter, in this case, was more like a handyman. It would be someone who would repair fences, doors, and other broken items.

Once again, I wonder what the angels thought when the one who spoke creation into existence was now relegated to a small shop, and instead of creating the beauty of the universe and the world, He was creating wooden items that he either fixed for others or made to sell to make money for the family.

He was born in a cattle stall. We can only imagine what the angels of heaven thought when they saw their creator bring born in a cattle stall. I would love to hear their thoughts when they saw his first bed was a feeding trough for the animals.

He was wrapped in swaddling clothes, which are rags used to wrap a newborn baby. There was no soft cotton or silk to clothe the newborn baby, only the strips of clothing gathered to wrap Jesus in.

It was a birth that was unnoticed by the population at large. In our culture, when a woman announces a pregnancy, the family and friends celebrate that announcement with her by giving baby showers and gifts to help with the newborn. Mary had none of that. There is even no indication that there was anyone to assist with the birth. She was on her own. No one seemed to notice or pay attention to the birth of Jesus.

Each of these historical details have spiritual implications

All of this information written by Luke provides very important lessons, both spiritual and historical. Luke presents the fact that Jesus was born alone with his parents in a cattle stall. He was born in poverty and unnoticed by the world.

Each of these facts have spiritual lessons for us. The fact that Jesus was born into poverty shows that God notices and cares for those who do not have great riches, live in large homes, or drive expensive cars. His birth into poverty was God saying that everyone, no matter who they are or what their social or economic standing is, God loves you, and God sent his son for you.

Those who are considered insignificant to the world are given grace and favor by God. The invitation he gives to the socially disadvantaged is the same invitation he gives to all. It does not matter if it is a rich young ruler who wants to know about eternal life, a Pharisee who wants to know about the new birth, or a woman who comes alone to get water at a well; the invitation is the same. **Come to Me and receive eternal life.** He wanted them to know that no social or economic position would prevent Him from loving them and desiring a relationship with them.

The second historical fact is that **when Mary and Joseph got to Bethlehem, there was no room for them.** This phrase used by Luke reveals the spiritual condition of the world. Just as there was no room for Jesus in an inn, there are many who have no room for Jesus in their lives. Their lives are filled with activities and pursuits that have an emphasis on the material things of the world, and they think little about their spiritual life. There are others who when they hear about Jesus, refuse to make room for Him in their lives. They are either too busy with the daily routine of their lives, or they choose to focus on the material rather than the spiritual.

Jesus was born at night which is a picture of the spiritual condition of the world. The world was in spiritual darkness, and the light of the world entered this darkness in a barn or cave in Bethlehem. The darkness indicated the hopelessness that people felt during this time. They were under the harsh rule of the Roman Empire. They were oppressed by the religious leaders, who imposed unnecessary burdens on the people.

The announcement of his birth was given first to Shepherds

Luke 2:8-14

And in the same region there were shepherds out in the field, keeping watch over their flock by night. And an angel of

the Lord appeared to them, and the glory of the Lord shone around them, and they were filled with great fear. And the angel said to them, "Fear not, for behold, I bring you good news of great joy that will be for all the people. For unto you is born this day in the city of David a Savior, who is Christ the Lord. And this will be a sign for you: you will find a baby wrapped in swaddling clothes and lying in a manger." And suddenly there was with the angel a multitude of the heavenly host praising God and saying, "Glory to God in the highest, and on earth peace among those with whom he is pleased!

The very first announcement of the birth of Jesus was made to men who were considered lowly, unclean, unreliable, and unimportant. They were generally excluded from worship services in the temple because they could not follow the traditions of cleanliness for worship. The world would expect an announcement of this significance to be made in the palaces where kings and queens reside. They thought it should have been made in the government halls where laws were made.

However, the angels in heaven did not appear in any of these important people or places. The angels appeared to those who were thought to be unworthy or unclean. There are many wonderful new lessons from the birth of Jesus, but the appearance of angels shows God's desire to reach all people, no matter their economic or social class. As far as God is concerned, the wealthiest and the lowliest are the same. He loves them the same, and He offers the same salvation to both.

After the Shepherds received the news from the angels, they immediately went to see this baby. One commentary suggests that the shepherds did not visit the baby because they did not believe the angels and wanted to verify their message. No, these Shepherds went because they believed what they were told. They went into Bethlehem expecting to see this one who was going to be the savior of the world.

Once they saw the baby with Mary and Joseph, they went back to their sheep, but they did not return to their work the same. They were changed by what they experienced and what they saw. As they returned to their flocks, they stopped everyone they could to tell them this incredible story. They saw angels, but more important than that they saw the savior of the world. They could not keep silent.

The announcement of the birth of Jesus was made by a Heavenly Choir.

It was not just one angel that made the announcement of the birth of Jesus. It was a host of angels. It appears that the birth of Jesus so stirred heaven that all of the angels wanted to get in on the celebration. Luke says **a host of angels appeared.** The word "host" can also be translated "army." (John Gill Commentary on Luke) Imagine that. The army of heaven is singing and they are celebrating that God is doing.

The message of the angels was a **message of great joy.** Not just joy but great joy. It was a great joy because God was addressing the spiritual condition of the world. He was opening the door for everyone to have an eternal relationship with Him.

It was great joy because God did not delegate this work of salvation to be done by any other but him. He did not assign this work to angels or other heavenly beings. He came Himself.

It was great joy because sin was going to be defeated once and for all. The power of sin was going to be taken away. This means that once Jesus is received as savior, sin does not have the power to change that relationship. Sin cannot remove us from being a child of God. Yes, it can still cause havoc in our lives if we let it, but it does not have the power to take away that new life God gave us.

The message was an announcement of peace on earth.

The peace that the angel is talking about here is not the absence of conflict. Our world is in a dangerous state of conflict as I write this: war between the Palestinians and Israel, war between Russia and Ukraine, conflict throughout the Middle East, and many other hot spots in the world. So, what did the angel mean when he spoke about peace on earth?

He is talking about the peace God has with those who receive the eternal life He offered to them. Peace on earth is about the peace we have with God. Before we became believers, our lives were in conflict with God, his laws, and his will. We were living a life of disobedience to Him. We were considered enemies of God. But not now. Now, we are different. Now, we are at peace with Him because He has forgiven us of our sins and has given us eternal life.

The message was delivered in the presence of the glory of the Lord.

Luke says that when the angels of the Lord appeared, **the glory of the Lord shone all around.** God's glory. God's glory is of two sorts: essential and declarative. The abasing nativity of Jesus Christ is the highest advancement of God's glory. This is a strange riddle to human reason, for God to raise His glory out of humiliation.

The glory referred to here is the visible, bright, illuminating glory of God. It is the glory that was witnessed by Moses, Joshua, Isaiah, Daniel, and the disciples on the Mount of Transfiguration. This is considered the **visible glory.**

There is another glory inferred here as well. It is the glory that comes with everything Jesus did in his life. John said in his letter, **We beheld His glory, the glory of the only begotten son of God.** This is more than just the glory seen during his transfiguration:

It is the glory of his wisdom. It was this wisdom that knew how to bring men into a relationship with God. Our own wisdom tried to find other ways to come to God. Some tried worship, doing good deeds, being a good person, etc. However, none of these things made it possible for us to have a relationship with God. Only one act could provide salvation, and that was God becoming a man. It was God taking upon himself our humanity, our sins, and our punishment. No one would have considered that this was the way to have a relationship with God. Our own intelligence says that there is something that we must do to have a relationship with God. The Bible says differently. The Bible says that our relationship with God is never dependent on what we do, but it is only dependent on what He does.

It is the glory of his demonstrated power. All of the gospel writers give multiple illustrations of the power of Jesus. He had the power over every kind of disease He encountered. He healed people who were diseased, blind, and crippled. He delivered men and women who were either possessed or oppressed by the demonic. All of these examples reveal just a portion of the power of Jesus. The greatest glory of his power is seen in what He does to a person who comes to Him for salvation. He takes a person who is dirty in sin and cleanses him from that sin. He takes a spiritual blind person and gives him spiritual sight. Most important of all, he demonstrates His power to take a sinner doomed for hell into a saint who is headed for heaven and the visible presence of God.

Conclusion

John says that **He beheld the glory of God.** We also get to see the glory of God. Not in the same way as John on the Mount of Transfiguration, but we see His glory in the lives of those who are living for him. If you are a believer, you are someone who reflects God's glory in your life. May we do what Jesus told us to do in the Sermon on the Mount: **Let your light so shine before men that they may see your good works AND GLORIFY YOUR FATHER IN HEAVEN. (Matthew 5:16)**

Chapter 9
The Glory of His Ministry

LUKE 4:14-30

16Then Jesus came to Nazareth, where He had been brought up. As was His custom, He entered the synagogue on the Sabbath. And when He stood up to read, 17the scroll of the prophet Isaiah was handed to Him. Unrolling it, He found the place where it was written:

18"The Spirit of the Lord is on Me,

because He has anointed Me

to preach good news to the poor.

He has sent Me to proclaim liberty to the captives*f*

and recovery of sight to the blind,

to release the oppressed,

19to proclaim the year of the Lord's favor."*g*

20Then He rolled up the scroll, returned it to the attendant, and sat down. The eyes of everyone in the synagogue were fixed on Him, 21and He began by saying, "Today this Scripture is fulfilled in your hearing."

22All spoke well of Him and marveled at the gracious words that came from His lips. "Isn't this the son of Joseph?" they asked.

23Jesus said to them, "Surely you will quote this proverb to Me: 'Physician, heal yourself! Do here in Your hometown what we have heard that You did in Capernaum.' "

24Then He added, "Truly I tell you, no prophet is accepted in his hometown. 25But I tell you truthfully that there were many widows in Israel in the time of Elijah, when the sky was shut for three and a half years and great famine swept over all the land. 26Yet Elijah was not sent to any of them, but to the widow of Zarephath in Sidon. 27And there were many lepers*h* in Israel in the time of Elisha the prophet. Yet not one of them was cleansed—only Naaman the Syrian."

28On hearing this, all the people in the synagogue were enraged. **29**They got up, drove Him out of the town, and led Him to the brow of the hill on which the town was built, in order to throw Him over the cliff. **30**But Jesus passed through the crowd and went on His way.

THE PRAISE AND THE POPULARITY OF JESUS

When Jesus came to Nazareth in this passage, the people were excited to see him. He had been gone for some time since he began his public ministry. The people were excited to see him because this was a hometown boy who did good. They remembered him when he was growing up in Nazareth. They remembered that he was a respectful young man. He never got into any kind of trouble. They remembered that he was the one who took care of his mother and his family when his father died. He left to begin a ministry. The word got back to town about how many wonderful things he was doing, and the people were looking forward to seeing him and hearing from him.

The Bible says that it was obvious that the power of God was on him. He was doing some remarkable work and teaching a wonderful message. Verse 14 says **The news about him spread all through the surrounding area.** The people of Nazareth eagerly anticipated hearing his teachings and witnessing his miracles. Surely, he would do some great work here. After all, this was his home. Many of the people were friends that he grew up with.

HIS EXAMPLE OF WORSHIP (16-19)

When Jesus came home to Nazareth, he did what he always did on the Sabbath day. He went to the synagogue to worship his Father. The NLT says **He went as usual.** In other words, this was the common practice of his life. One of the great tragedies today is that there are so many Christians who do not feel the need to worship the Lord on Sunday. They can come up with all kinds of excuses as to why it is not necessary for them to spend time in church. I have heard many people say to me I don't have to be in church to worship the Lord. And they are correct. They don't have to be in church to worship the Lord, but if we do not worship the Lord with God's people on the Lord's Day, then two things happen.

When we refuse to spend time in worship with God's people, then we are being disobedient to the Lord. We are outside of his will for our lives. God did not save us and then say that it was okay to live independently of the church. He did not save us and then say that we could grow spiritually without cooperate worship. He saved us to be a part of a fellowship of believers. To refuse to do that is to be disobedient to him. The Bible says, **Do not forsake the assembling of yourselves together.** To refuse to do so is to be outside of the will of God for our spiritual growth.

The second thing that happens is that we hinder the work of the Holy Spirit to make us into the image of Jesus. The reason for our salvation was that God wanted to make us like his son. He wants to conform us to his image. If we are going to be like Jesus, one of the things that involves is worship and fellowship with the people of God. This verse says that Jesus went to the synagogue as was his usual practice. He felt the need to attend worship and Bible study with the people of God. If Jesus, the Son of God, felt the need to worship, how then can we think that we don't need it or can do without it? If we are going to become like Christ, may worship with God's people be the faithful activity of our life.

THE SERMON OF JESUS

Jesus was asked by the attendant of the synagogue to preach the sermon for that day. We are familiar with this practice in that when a young man is called to the ministry from our church; he is sometimes invited to preach at his home church. We want to hear from him and how he is doing. Or when someone is called to the mission field. We want to hear about their ministry and what kind of experiences they are having. This was the case in this passage of scripture.

The Bible says that Jesus opens the scroll of Isaiah and reads Isaiah 61:1,2 and 58:6 with a couple of lines left out. After He reads the scripture, He then goes and sits down. This is the position of the teacher or the preacher. The people stood, and the preacher sat down. His sermon is simple but shocking. Jesus reads the passage concerning what the Messiah is going to do when he comes.

The people of Israel were looking for the Messiah. They were waiting for him to come and deliver Israel from the bondage of the Romans. They were waiting for someone to come and restore the great power of Israel as it was under King David and Solomon. Jesus reads the passage of scripture that lets them know the Messiah is not going to be a political king, but he is going to be a spiritual king. The Messiah is not going to deliver them from political bondage, but he is going to deliver them from Spiritual bondage. He then lists this spiritual ministry the Messiah is to do.

The passage He reads reveals the power and the authority given to Him by the Spirit of the Lord.

He reads **The spirit of the Lord is upon me and has anointed me.** He begins by letting his listeners know that He is not here on his own authority, but He is here by the authority of God. He has been appointed to this task. His interpretation of this Isaiah passage was different than how the religious leaders interpreted it. Most of the rabbis believed that this passage was referring to the coming of a future king in Israel. They believed that the Messiah was going to be one who would deliver them from the oppression of Rome and restore Israel to the glory days of David and Solomon.

When Jesus said that He was the anointed one, it caused quite a stir among those who were listening. It was disturbing to those who heard Him say that because they remembered Him as a boy growing up in Nazareth. They remember His parents. So, in their minds, how could this man from Nazareth be the Messiah? How could He be the Messiah?

The Hebrews were very familiar with the phrase "Anointed One." Throughout their history, kings, priests, and prophets were called "The Lords Anointed." These were men who were considered chosen by God to do the work of God. The visible expression of being chosen by God was to be anointed with oil. Oil, which represents the presence of God, was poured over the head of the one chosen. The individual then became known as the "chosen of God."

Jesus declares that He is the Anointed One. He is the one chosen by God to usher in the kingdom of God. Jesus was not anointed in the same way as Old Testament leaders were. He gave reference to his anointing when he said **the spirit of the Lord is upon me.** He was not anointed with oil but with the Spirit Himself. When he read that passage, He may have been thinking of His baptism. The Bible says that when Jesus was baptized, **the Holy Spirit came down in bodily shape, like a dove on Him. And a voice came from Heaven saying, You are my son in whom I am well pleased. (Luke 3:22).**

By claiming that he was the Anointed One, He was declaring that He was the Christ. He was the Messiah. He was the one God anointed to be a Prophet, Priest, and King. God set Him apart to do this work. This passage indicates that he was not the kind of king they were expecting. He was not going to set up a physical or political kingdom. He was going to set up the kingdom of the heart and soul. He was going to set up a kingdom that had no geographical boundaries. He was not going to be building an army to overthrow Rome; he was building a kingdom that would overcome sin, death, and the grave.

Yes, he would raise an army, but it was not going to be an army like Rome; it would be a spiritual army. His army would have weapons, swords, and shields, but they would be spiritual weapons. The sword they would carry would be the sword of the Word of God.

Even though the people were expecting a king like Caesar, they were going to get a king who had a different agenda. They were not going to get a king who wanted to expand national boundaries. Instead, they were going to get a king who changed the hearts and lives of men and women who believed in Him. He then explains how His kingdom will grow. It will grow through His preaching and teaching.

He came to preach the gospel or the good news.

He came to preach the gospel to the poor. The word " poor is not a reference to material or financial poverty. It is a reference to the spiritual poverty of a person. It is a word that means to cringe or to crouch in a begging manner. It is to bend down, bow your head, and hold out your hands. It is a word which speaks of an **attitude of the mind.** It means to realize that I am utterly helpless. It means that I am completely empty. There is nothing in me that is worth anything.

Jesus said that He came to preach the gospel or the good news to those who were in this spiritual poverty. He came to preach about the spiritual riches available to all of those who were impoverished in their relationship with God. He came to fill the emptiness, to give worth and value to the worthless, and to make rich those who had nothing.

I think about how many people I have met in my life who are just empty. They feel overwhelmed by their spiritual poverty. Nothing they have tried or experienced makes them feel any better. Nothing they have tried gives them a sense of fulfillment. These men and women need good news. They need to hear that Jesus is the wonderful answer to the emptiness in their lives.

He came to proclaim release to the captives. The word captive refers to a prisoner of war who has been dragged away by the enemy. We have all heard about or read about men and women who were held captive by a cruel enemy. Those who told these stories told about how they were mistreated and abused. Many were starved, tortured, and physically maimed.

As I write this, the Nation of Israel is recovering from a horrendous attack by the terrorist group HAMMAS. On October 7, 2023, HAMMAS brutally attacked a Jewish community where hundreds of men, women, and children were killed, beheaded, and burned alive. Hostages were taken, and now Israel is in an all-out war to destroy HAMMAS but also to deliver those who were captured. They are doing everything they can to bring those hostages home alive.

I read about the efforts being made to find these men, women, and children and bring them home. Families of the victims are filled with fear and anxiety that their loved ones will not make it home alive.

All of the efforts to bring home these hostages are tremendous and as great as these efforts are, they are nothing in comparison to what Jesus did to deliver those who were captured by sin. The effort it took to deliver men and women from sin was a cross. It took His death, the death of the Son of God on the cross to free us from sin.

Jeremiah Denton was a pilot who was shot down in Vietnam. He was held prisoner for 7 1/2 years. After he was released, he wrote a book entitled WHEN HELL WAS IN SESSION. In this book, he tells of brutality and torture that is hard to read. He shares that the purpose of all that brutality was to break him and his fellow prisoners to speak out against the United States. When these prisoners refused to do that, they were beaten, starved, and a host of other atrocities. I think the title of his book is appropriate. When men are being brutalized in the ways described in his book, it does seem that God is absent and Hell is in control. (When Hell was in Session, Admiral Jeremiah Denton, WMD Publisher, November 2009)

There are many kinds of spiritual bondage that men and women experience other than being taken captive by some enemy force. Some are captives to the love of money and materialism. Their thoughts are always on making money and living with the fear of losing money. I watched a News program where there was a round table discussion on what people were afraid of. Each participant went around the table and talked about their fears. One of the participants said that the thing he feared the most was losing his money and being poor. He talked about how he watched the stock market every day to make sure he was not losing money. He would get up in the middle of the night to see if everything was alright. He lives with the anxiety of all he might lose.

Some are captives to sensuality; some are captives of hatred, racism, and greed. Some have become captive to drugs or alcohol. There are many different kinds of captivity today, and all of them are horrible. Jesus said that he came to proclaim release to those who are being held captive.

He came to free every person who is in bondage to anything that drags them down. He came to bring release to every person whose life is miserable because of some spiritual condition. He came to set the prisoner free.

He came to minister to those who were in need:

He came to heal the brokenhearted: He did not come just to help the brokenhearted; he came to heal them. I have a feeling that the same things that broke the hearts of men and women during Jesus' time on earth are the same things that break hearts today.

Some are broken hearted because of a grief they have experienced. Some lost loved ones. Some are going through a divorce. Some are having problems with their children. Everything they have done does not seem to work. They are brokenhearted. Jesus came to heal that broken heart.

Some are broken hearted because of sin and failure in their lives. Each of us have a desire to live before the Lord in a way that honors him. We want to be known as someone who is truly a Christian. But we sin. We fail. For some of us, we have been wrestling with a certain sin for a long time and it always seems to get the best of us. We are brokenhearted because we do not have victory over those sins.

Some are brokenhearted because they feel alone and isolated.

Some are broken hearted because of finances. They don't have enough money to pay their bills. They are overwhelmed with financial burdens.

Some are broken hearted because they have not recovered from storms that destroyed their homes and uprooted their lives.

Some are brokenhearted because they have been abandoned by a spouse.

Jesus said that he came to heal the brokenhearted. He came to help us feel better and be stronger in our present circumstances. How, then, does He do that? The healing comes through our being united with Him. He brings us to Himself and gives us a sense of his love and presence. Being joined to Him, is the bandage needed for our spiritual wounds.

Being united with Him does not mean we will never again have sadness in our life. It does not mean we are going to avoid everything that can hurt us. Jesus never promised that following Him was going to be an easy task. He never said that we will never be sick, never lose a loved one, never be betrayed, or other heartbreaking experiences we have. He did say that in all of those circumstances He would be with us. He did say that He would never leave us alone. Even in those times when our emotions are frayed because of heartbreak, and we can't feel his presence, He is still with us. When we feel He is distant and we can't find Him, he is always near and working to bring healing in every heartbreaking experience we have.

He came to give sight to the blind: This has two meanings. He wanted to give sight to those who were physically blind, and the second meaning and most important one is that he wanted to give sight to those who were spiritually blind. He wanted to open their eyes to their spiritual condition without him. He wanted them to see and understand his word. He wanted them to see their sinful condition. He wanted them to see their emptiness and what was causing it. He wanted to give sight to the blind.

He came to give liberty to the oppressed. The word for oppressed means to be broken in pieces. It means to be crushed under a heavy weight. The greatest oppression that any person has is the oppression of sin. It is to be crushed by failure, shame, sin, and other problems. Jesus said the Messiah would give liberty to those who were oppressed.

He came to preach God's grace and salvation, not condemnation or judgment. If you go back and read the entire verse that Jesus read from, you will find out that he left out part of it. The end of Isaiah 61:1 speaks of the judgment of God. Jesus left that out. Jesus was not diminishing the judgment of God. He spent his ministry talking about God's judgment in the context of one's relationship to Jesus. Those who believe in Jesus will not be condemned, but those who do reject him will face eternal condemnation.

Jesus said that he came to **proclaim the favorable year of the Lord.** This refers to the time when God is willing to accept men and women who come to him. It is that time when he is willing to receive sinners and forgive them of their sins. This is that time of grace. It is that time when God allows guilty men and women to return to him. When they do, they will be received. This is what Jesus came to preach. He came to preach that there is now an opportunity to find forgiveness with God. There is now the opportunity to be saved.

However, the implication is that there will be a time when this age will end. There will be a time when God will not receive sinners. There will be a time when God will not forgive the guilty. God said to Noah in the Old Testament, **my spirit will not always contend with man.** In other words, my spirit will not always convict and encourage men to be saved. So, while the opportunity is here, those who are Christians must preach the good news, and those who are lost must receive it.

THE CLAIM OF JESUS

After Jesus read from the scripture, He sat down and looked at the people. The Bible says that there was a sense of eager expectation. What would he say? It had been reported that he was a wonderful teacher and a wonderful preacher. What kind of sermon would he preach today? The Bible says, **all eyes were fixed on him.** They were giving full attention to what Jesus was saying.

Luke does not give us the details of the sermon Jesus preached. He does give us the central theme. As Jesus was speaking, he made the most remarkable claim that any of them ever heard. He shocked them with the statement, **today this scripture is fulfilled in your hearing.**

Jesus was saying to them that he was the one that Isaiah spoke about. He was the one in which this scripture was fulfilled. Many people read the Bible and argue that Jesus never claimed to be the Messiah. This is one of those passages that proves them wrong. Here, in this text, Jesus claimed to be the Messiah, the one they were expecting to come from God. He was letting them know that the coming of the Messiah was not going to happen in the future; it happened now, today. All of the scripture of Isaiah was fulfilled in him.

Jesus claimed that:

that He was the One upon whom the Spirit dwelt

that He was the One anointed to preach the gospel to the poor and captives.

that He was the One who healed the brokenhearted.

that He was the One who gave sight to the blind.

that He was the One who freed the bruised.

that He was the One who preached the acceptable year of the Lord, the age of salvation.

This was not the only place where Jesus claimed to be the Messiah.

"He saith unto them, But whom say ye that I am? And Simon Peter answered and said, Thou art the Christ, the Son of the living God. And Jesus answered and said unto him, Blessed art thou, Simon Barjona: for flesh and blood hath not revealed it unto thee, but my Father which is in heaven" (Matthew 15:16-17)

Notice that when Peter confessed that Jesus was the Christ, Jesus did not deny it. He did not tell Peter he was wrong. He accepted the confession.

"The woman saith unto him, I know that Messiah comes which is called Christ: when he is come, he will tell us all things. Jesus saith unto her, I that speak unto thee am he" (John 4:35-36)

"Jesus said unto her, I am the resurrection, and the life: he that believes in me, though he were dead, yet shall he live: and whosoever liveth and believes in me shall never die. (John 11:35-37)

These are just a few of the passages we can find where Jesus points out that he is the Messiah. Why is this important to know? It is important because of what Isaiah said he would do. There is no other religious leader who ever claimed to be able to heal the brokenhearted. No other religious leader ever claimed to be able to open the eyes of the blind. None of them claimed to do these things. And so if a person wants to be set free, if he wants to have insight into what is important in life, if he wants to be healed of guilt and shame or any other kind of problem, the only person he can come to is Jesus. The only place to turn is Jesus. This is why it is important to know who he is.

The question we all have to ask ourselves is, do I have a personal relationship with this savior?

What do we really know about Jesus?

When we come to the Christmas season, we begin to focus on what is the most important event in all of history. It is the event of God becoming a man. When I speak of the event, I am not just talking about his birth, but I am speaking about his whole human life, his birth, his ministry, his teachings, his miracles and his death, burial and resurrection, and finally, his ascension. This is the greatest event in all of the world.

Chapter 10
The Glory of Jesus Human Education

Job 10:1-5

I know that this is an unusual title for a chapter. What kind of education did Jesus have to go through to be the savior of the world? When Jesus was a young boy, he would have been taught the Torah by the various rabbis. He would have been taught about the Jewish traditions. This is not the education I am referring to here. It is not the education of a school that studies the scripture.

The education I am referring to is the education of life, the kind that everyone can relate to. Jesus had to learn things that were not in books. He had to experience things that books did not talk about. He had to learn how to be an older brother and how to take care of his family after his father died. He had to learn what it was to be hungry or grow tired. He had to learn about disappointment and betrayal. This was his lifelong learning curve, one that we all navigate in our own ways.

Job is asking these kinds of questions.

1 "I am disgusted with my life. Let me complain freely. My bitter soul must complain.

2 I will say to God, 'Don't simply condemn me— tell me the charge you are bringing against me.

3 What do you gain by oppressing me? Why do you reject me, the work of your own hands, while smiling on the schemes of the wicked?

4 Are your eyes like those of a human? Do you see things only as people see them?

5 Is your lifetime only as long as ours? Is your life so short

6 that you must quickly probe for my guilt and search for my sin?

7 Although you know I am not guilty, no one can rescue me from your hands.

Those who know the story of Job know that God was allowing him to go through some very severe testing. He lost his family, his wealth, and his health in a very short period of time. In one of those low moments of his suffering, he complains to God about what is going on, and then he asks this question: **Are your eyes like those of a human; is your lifetime as long as ours?**

Do you realize what Job is asking? He is asking, Lord, do you really know what is going on? Do you really know how I feel and how I hurt? You do not have a body like mine. You don't have pain like mine. There is no way that you can know how I feel.

Job is not the only one who questions God about this. Moses, Jeremiah, and some of the Psalmists believed that God did not know what they were going through. He could not know because he was God, and he was not a human being.

All of that changed on Christmas. God suddenly found out what it was like to be human. He found out what it was like to be confined by time, space, and knowledge. Jesus experienced the human experience completely and fully. As a young man, he experienced the grief of loss. His father, Joseph, died, and since Jesus was the oldest son, he became responsible for taking care of his family. He learned what it took to make ends meet. Jesus, the one who had unlimited riches in glory, now finds that he has to work long hours and many jobs in order to provide food for his family. He learned what it meant to be the breadwinner for His family.

Throughout his life, he experienced emotions and circumstances that He never experienced in heaven. Jesus couldn't experience the things that we do as long as He was in heaven. When He became a man, he then truly learned the human experience.

He learned what it was **to be hungry and tired and thirsty.** John 4 He asked a woman for a drink. After feeding the 5000, he was so tired that he fell into a deep sleep in a boat that was being rocked about by strong winds and waves crashing into the boat. He was so fatigued that the storm did not wake Him up.

He learned what it was like **to experience pain, sorrow, and loneliness**. He found out what it was like to be **disappointed** by the people you love and those who love you. He then found out what it was like to die.

Job asked the question: **do you have eyes of flesh?** When Jesus came, God could answer, yes, I do have eyes of flesh. I do see things as other humans do. For 33 years, Jesus lived, worked, and ministered as a man doing the work of God;

Jesus also learned to interact with men and women on a human level. He could look them in the eye. He could reach out and touch them, and they could touch him. His interaction with people was gentle when healing and firm when correction was needed.

The Old Testament documents how God interacted with people in a completely different way. He did not interact with them as a human being but as God. He spoke to Moses out of a burning bush. He spoke to Job out of a whirlwind. He spoke to Isaiah in visions. He spoke to Daniel through visions and dreams. In each of these experiences, God was untouchable. He could not be looked at because of the fullness of His glory. All that changed on Christmas. God becoming a man radically changed how He interacted with us. When Jesus was born, God was making himself visible in the life of Jesus. Jesus said He who has seen me has seen the Father. So, as God in the flesh, the interactions, the communications, and the blessings came from one who was with us. He was present. His presence allowed us to see the glory of God. According to the writer of Hebrews, the coming of Jesus was the final way in which God spoke to man. If there is to be any connection to God the Father, it comes through a relationship with Jesus. If there is any communication, he does so through Jesus in our lives.

Hebrews 1:1-2.

1 Long ago, God spoke many times and in many ways to our ancestors through the prophets.

2 And now, in these final days, he has spoken to us through his Son. God promised everything to the Son as an inheritance, and through the Son, he created the universe.

Jesus experiencing the human condition is one miracle. The idea of God becoming a man is truly remarkable to think about. Still, there is another miracle to consider. Jesus fully lived out the human experience. He learned about pain, sorrow, and disappointment. He also learned about the verbal and physical attacks on those who wanted to kill Him. Everything Jesus went through in the human experience was traumatic on many levels. Jesus experienced the hardships of being human but did not sin.

He grew up with brothers and sisters and did not sin. He became responsible for taking care of His family when His father died and did not complain about it. He felt grief because He knew that his disciples, all of them, were going to reject Him and run away. He knew Jesus was going to betray Him, and Peter was going to deny Him. Knowing these things, he did not become angry or demeaning to those who were prophesied to fail. He just knelt down and washed their feet.

The Bible teaches that God became a man to restore the human race to a right relationship with him. He became a man so he could live a perfect, sinless life and then pay the price for the sins of the world.

The Bible teaches that Jesus died on the cross. His death on the cross was more than just some criminal dying; it was the God-Man taking upon himself all of the sins of the world. In those six hours on the cross, God poured out all of his wrath on Jesus because of the sins that others committed.

Isaiah 53:3-6 describes this event on the cross.

3 He was despised and rejected— a man of sorrows, acquainted with deepest grief. We turned our backs on him and looked the other way. He was despised, and we did not care.

4 Yet it was our weaknesses he carried; it was our sorrows that weighed him down. And we thought his troubles were a punishment from God, a punishment for his own sins!

5 But he was pierced for our rebellion, crushed for our sins. He was beaten so we could be whole. He was whipped so we could be healed.

6 All of us, like sheep, have strayed away. We have left God's paths to follow our own. Yet the Lord laid on him the sins of us all.

7 He was oppressed and treated harshly, yet he never said a word. He was led like a lamb to the slaughter. And as a sheep is silent before the shearers, he did not open his mouth.

When people walked by the cross and witnessed the suffering of Jesus and the other two thieves dying with Him, they assumed that this was just another criminal being executed. They just looked at Him as another criminal being crucified.

When witnesses saw his suffering and his pain, they thought that he was such a bad person that God was punishing him severely. The truth of the matter was that, yes, God was punishing him. Yes, God was pouring out his wrath on him.

This punishment and this outpouring of wrath was not for anything Jesus did, but it was for everything we had done. God was punishing him for our sins and for our rebellion and disobedience.

This suffering paid the price for our sins and provided salvation for all those who believe in Him. The suffering brought reconciliation to those who were lost in sin. This suffering provided a pathway to heaven.

This is the Jesus of scripture. This is how the Bible describes Jesus. Even though the scripture is very clear on who Jesus is, what He did and why he did it. The scripture described Him as a sinless man satisfying the wrath of God. Even though the scripture is clear in its presentation of Jesus, many people in the world have differing opinions about who He is. Many consider Him a good man who was crucified because He defied the Roman governments and the Jewish religious authorities. He is thought of as a good teacher but not the savior of the world. Others consider Him to be equal to Buddha, Mohammed, and other religious leaders.

Think about your vision or your understanding of Jesus. When you hear his name, what kind of vision comes to your mind? What does he look like? How is he dressed? How does he speak to the crowds or to the individuals?

You might think that is a strange question, but in reality, the kind of Jesus that we picture in our minds is the kind of Jesus that we will imitate or the kind of Jesus that we will obey.

The way Jesus has been presented to the world.

In considering some of the things that have been written about Jesus and some of the movies produced about him, the presentations have very little resemblance to the Jesus found in the gospel.

Consider for a moment some of the books that have been written about Jesus. Some Christian athletes picture Jesus as some kind of sports star, some kind of all-American athlete.

Norm Evans, a former Miami Dolphin lineman, wrote a book called <u>On God's Squad.</u> In his book, he describes Jesus as someone who would be the toughest guy to ever play the game. Evan's wrote If Jesus were alive, I would picture him as a six foot six inch 260-pound tackle who would always make big plays and be hard to keep out of the backfield.

Fritz Peterson, a former New York Yankee, thinks about Jesus in a baseball uniform. He says, **I firmly believe that if Jesus Christ were sliding into second base, he would knock the second baseman into left field and break up a double play…he would play hard within the rules.**

Others have pictured Jesus as a modern-day hippie going around in a robe, wearing sandals, and eating only vegetables.

And then there are others who try to degrade or blaspheme the name of Jesus. Dan Brown, in his book <u>The Davinci Code</u>, says that Jesus was married to Mary Magdalene before he died and had children.

Another playwright says that Jesus was a homosexual who had relations with his twelve disciples.

Another wrote in **the Passover plot** that the whole experience of the death, burial, and resurrection of Jesus was nothing more than a farce. Jesus did not really die on the cross. He just passed out, and the disciples took him down before he died. He was placed in a tomb where the cool air revived him, and he moved away the stone and left the tomb, and his disciples said that he was resurrected.

Some see Jesus as a heavenly Santa Claus that gives us everything that we ask for.

Some see Jesus as being so compassionate that he just accepts everything and does not ever condemn of judge anyone.

The way Jesus is presented in the Bible

1. In Humility:

He was born in humility in a barn

He was born to humble, impoverished parents

He was revealed to nobodies: Shepherds who did not even leave their names when they visited Jesus in the manger.

He worked as a carpenter.

No one expected God to come in such a humble state; most believed God would come in majesty and glory.

2. He was approachable

In most religions, God is approached with great fear. The Muslims, for instance, bow so low in their worship that their heads touch the ground

The Jews approached God with fear as they worshipped him. They were afraid that they might offend him, and he might retaliate.

Jesus, the God=Man was approachable

by little children

by untouchable lepers

by religious leaders at night

by the demon possessed.

by a dying thief on a cross

by a doubting disciple, Thomas

By you and me for salvation

3. He was compassionate

He had compassion on the sick

He had compassion on the multitudes because he considered them to be sheep without a shepherd or a leader.

He had compassion on you and me because of the lost condition of our lives.

4. He was forgiving

He forgave Peter for denying him.

He forgave the thief on the cross.

He forgave Zachaeus for his corruption.

He forgave his disciples for running away.

He forgave the woman at the well.

He forgave the woman caught in adultery.

He forgave you and me for every sin that we committed.

5. He was courageous

He faced the religious leaders and called them hypocrites for the way they were living their lives.

He accepted the cross when he was in the garden of Gethsemane, asking to find another way.

He stood courageously silent before Pilate and all of those who accused him.

He was courageous to all of those who followed him, looking for something that they might accuse him of.

6. He was a warrior

He came to fight the battle of the ages. He came to fight death, hell, the grave, and Satan.

He died, but then he rose again.

He descended into hell, but he led captivity captive and delivered all of those Old Testament saints into the presence of God.

He went into a grave, but three days later, he knocked the door away and said that the grave no longer had the final word. The final word rested in the victory of Jesus Christ in the resurrection.

He defeated Satan once and for all. He removed the power of the devil in that he no longer has any power over anyone who enters into a personal relationship with Jesus Christ.

7. He was a man of great joy.

He had joy the world does not have, and the world does not understand. It is the joy of knowing that all things are in the hands of God and he is working out everything according to his will.

He had joy beyond the cross. This is what the writer of Hebrews referred to. He said that one of the reasons that Jesus went to the cross was because of the joy that awaited him on the other side. He had the joy of victory and the joy of returning to the glory he had with the Father.

He has joy at the conversion of those who are lost. The Bible says that there is joy in the midst of the angels of heaven when someone is saved. It is Jesus who is joyful because another has been saved from sin and is given eternal life.

8. He was a man of great zeal and passion.

He was passionate about his Father's house

He was passionate about the mistreatment of the poor and the helpless.

He was passionate about exposing hypocrisy

He was passionate about doing his Father's will.

9. He condemned intentional sinful behavior.

10. He was a man of sorrow.

Sorrow for the rejection of his people

Sorrow for unbelief in others

Sorrow for the lost condition of the multitudes.

Conclusion:

The coming of Jesus on Christmas Day is a story like no other. It is the story of the creator descending to this small, insignificant planet to give you and me eternal life. It was this event that revealed:

The glory of God.

The love of God

The power of God.

At the same time, the coming of Jesus answered all of the questions that Job had about God.

4 Are your eyes like those of a human? Do you see things only as people see them?

5 Is your lifetime only as long as ours? Is your life so short

6 that you must quickly probe for my guilt and search for my sin

Do you have the eyes of a human? Yes, I do. I became a man so I could see the world through human eyes.

Do you see things only as people see them? No He does not see things just like ordinary people. He sees things in their completeness. He sees the heart and mind. He sees the attitudes and the motives for doing things. He sees the grief even when it's being hidden. He sees the hurt when a sick person touches Him. No, He does not see things like people. Instead, he sees things as the God-man.

Is your lifetime only as long as ours? The answer to this question is more difficult to answer. His life as a human being was short. He lived only about 33 years. He died as a young man. Three days later, He rose, but He rose in his human body, but it was a changed body. It was a glorified body. In this body, he carries the scars from the nails on his hands and feet. He carries the wound on his side.

However, this body now is different. This body can never die. This body can never feel pain anymore. He leaves behind all of these human experiences. His resurrected body will never experience any of these things again. His resurrection is a picture of what kind of body we will have at our resurrection. We, too, will have a body that no longer experiences pain, gets sick with a terminal disease, and suffers from various illnesses. This is the kind of body we look forward to having.

We have a savior who can say, I understand everything you are going through. I know everything you're going through, not because I witnessed it or watched you but because I experienced those things. I know what terrible temptation is like. I know what physical pain is.

I know about betrayal. Jesus would say I became a man so. You could be with me and like me.

Chapter 11
The Glory and The Power of The Cross

As has been stated throughout this study is that the primary theme of all scripture is the coming of Jesus into the world to save us from our sins. However, the emphasis on Jesus' coming was how He was going to be able to do that. How was Jesus going to save us from our sins? The answer found throughout scripture is THE CROSS. Jesus was going to save us from sin by paying the price for our sins on the cross. Dying on a cross was one of the worst kinds of death a person could experience. Not only did it involve the pain of having nails driven into hands and feet, but the way a person was positioned on the cross meant that he was going to experience the pain of suffocation. The lungs would fill up with fluid and blood, and eventually, the victim could not take in breath. It was a slow, agonizing death, and that was the kind of death Jesus experienced so you and I could have eternal life.

The prophet Isaiah was given a picture of the kind of death Jesus would experience on the cross.

He was despised and rejected by men, a man of sorrows and acquainted with grief, and as one from whom men hide their faces, he was despised, and we esteemed him not. Surely, he has borne our griefs and carried our sorrows, yet we esteemed him stricken, smitten by God, and afflicted. But he was pierced for our transgressions; he was crushed for our iniquities; upon him was the chastisement that brought us peace, and with his wounds, we are healed. All we like sheep have gone astray; we have turned—everyone—to his own way; and the LORD has laid on him the iniquity of us all. He was oppressed, and he was afflicted, yet he opened not his mouth; like a lamb that is led to the slaughter, and like a sheep that before its shearers is silent, so he opened not his mouth. By oppression and judgment, he was taken away, and as for his generation, who considered that he was cut off out of the land of the living, stricken for the transgression of my people? And they made his grave with the wicked and with a rich man in his death,

although he had done no violence, and there was no deceit in his mouth. Yet it was the will of the LORD to crush him; he has put him to grief; when his soul makes an offering for guilt, he shall see his offspring; he shall prolong his days; the will of the LORD shall prosper in his hand. Out of the anguish of his soul he shall see and be satisfied; by his knowledge shall the righteous one, my servant, make many to be accounted righteous, and he shall bear their iniquities. Therefore, I will divide him a portion with the many, and he shall divide the spoil with the strong because he poured out his soul to death and was numbered with the transgressors; yet he bore the sin of many and makes intercession for the transgressors. (Isaiah 53:3-11 ESV)

What an amazing prophecy here. Jesus not only experienced the physical torture of dying on the cross, but he also experienced mental and emotional anguish as well.

He was despised and rejected. Why? Every page in the gospels talks about how Jesus loved people, had compassion on them, healed them, and fed them when they were hungry. Many people witnessed the miracles He performed, including raising someone from the dead. He was gentle with the worst of sinners. He never turned anyone away that came to Him. Considering all of these wonderful things that Jesus did, how then can the people of his day despise Him. How could they reject someone who was so full of goodness, grace, and compassion?

He carried our weakness. I think about my own life and consider the continual sins I committed. Some of these sins of mine would be considered besetting sins. These are sins that keep asserting themselves in our lives. These are sins, we tend to commit over and over again even though we pray and ask the Lord to help us overcome them. These besetting sins are our weakness. Isaiah says that **He carried our weakness.** He carried those sins that have been disruptive in our lives and paid the price for them. Jesus suffered this agonizing death so these repeated, besetting sins could be defeated in our lives.

Isaiah goes into descriptive detail of the kind of treatment Jesus received because of our sins.

He was wounded, crushed, beaten, and whipped so we could have everlasting life. (5).

He was oppressed and treated harshly (6)

It was the Lord's plan to crush Him and fill Him with grief (10)

This description of Jesus' death was written hundreds of years before Jesus was born. When we read the gospel accounts of Jesus' death on the cross, He experienced everything that Isaiah mentioned. His death was filled with such agony that you and I can't imagine the physical, emotional, and mental pain Jesus went through. And it was this cross that the gospel writers focused on. There is very little information available about His childhood or early ministry. They talked about the cross and His crucifixion. The writers of the rest of the New Testament also focused on the death of Jesus on the cross. In 1 Corinthians 1:23, Paul said when we preach that Christ was crucified, the Jews are offended, **and the Gentiles say that it is nonsense.**

In 1 Corinthians 2:2, Paul says, **For I decided to focus on Jesus Christ and His death on the cross.**

Galatians 6:14 says **But far be it from me to boast except in the cross of our Lord Jesus Christ, by which the world has been crucified to me, and I to the world.**

The writers of the New Testament concentrated their teaching, preaching, and writing on the cross of Jesus. They knew that salvation did not come through the birth of Jesus, the miracles of Jesus, or any story about his childhood or family. They knew that the only way a person could be saved from their sin was through the death of Jesus on the cross. They focused on the cross because it was the cross that radically changed their lives.

It is also the cross of Jesus that radically changes everything about us. It was the cross that changed our relationship with God. He is now our Father, and we are His children. It is the cross that changed our relationship with the world. We no longer have the same relationship with the world because of the cross. We are now **strangers and aliens** in the world because of what the cross did to us and for us. We no longer belong to the world, but we now belong to the kingdom of God. Because we belong to the Kingdom of God, we are **ambassadors for Christ.** We now represent Jesus and his kingdom.

We are ambassadors for Christ in a hostile world. The world refuses to believe that Jesus is God in the flesh. The world refuses to believe that Jesus is the only way to heaven. The message we bring to the world is not an all-inclusive message. Jesus is not one god among many gods. He is not one way among many ways to get to heaven. He is the only way. This message that Jesus is the only way to heaven is perceived as a threat to all other religious beliefs. This is why Christians have been and are being persecuted in the world. The world hates the message of Christ because it proclaims the exclusivity of Jesus as the only way to salvation.

Because the world hates the message of the cross, it also hates those who preach and teach about the cross. The message of the cross not only has the power to change individuals, but it also has the power to change governments, education, and social policies and destroy other religious thinking. Jesus prepared His disciples for the kind of hostility and persecution they would face because of the gospel. He warned them that in this world, they would face persecution because of the gospel.

In Matthew 10, Jesus said, **Behold, I am sending you out as sheep in the midst of wolves, so be wise as serpents and innocent as doves. Beware of men, for they will deliver you over to courts and flog you in their synagogues, and you will be dragged before governors and kings for my sake, to bear witness before them and the Gentiles. When they deliver you over, do not be anxious how you are to speak or what you are to say, for what you are to say will be given to you in that hour. For it is not you who speak, but the Spirit of your Father speaking through you. Brother will deliver brother over to death, and the father his child, and children will rise against parents and have them put to death, and you will be hated by** all for my name's sake. But the one who endures to the end will be saved. (Matthew 10:16-23. NKJV). Because of our faith in Jesus, the world considers us to be their enemy.

The cross is the central theme of our resurrected Lord. When Jesus reveals His glory to John in the book of Revelation, Jesus emphasized the cross. John to the seven churches that are in Asia: Grace to you and peace from him who is and who was and who is to come, and from the seven spirits who are before his throne, and from Jesus Christ the faithful witness, the firstborn of the dead, and the ruler of kings on earth. To him who loves us and has freed us from our sins by his blood. And made us a kingdom, priests to his God and Father, to him be glory and dominion forever and ever. Amen. Behold, he is coming with the clouds, and every eye will see him, even those who pierced him, and all tribes of the earth will wail on account of him. Even so. Amen. "I am the Alpha and the Omega," says the Lord God, "who is and who was and who is to come, the Almighty." (Revelation 1:4-9)

Notice how Jesus says that the world will see Him when He returns. In verse 6, he says, every eye will see Him, EVEN THOSE WHO PIERCED HIM. (NKJV). This, of course, refers to the nails driven into his hands and his feet. He not only refers to the nails, but He also says that He washed us with his own blood.

The cross is also the central focus in heaven. All of the living beings in heaven rejoice because of the cross of Jesus. They recognize that the work of Jesus on the cross is the most radical work He ever did. The angels rejoice, the elders sing praise and bow down, and all the others in heaven praise God because of the cross. When the saints of God get to heaven, each of us are going to recognize in a most perfect way that we are able to be there because of the cross of Jesus.

Revelation 5:6-9 says, And I When he was at living creatures and in the midst of the elders stood a lamb as though it had been slain having seven horns and seven eyes which are the seven spirits of God sent out into the world. And they sang a new song, saying, "Worthy are you to take the scroll and to open its seals, for you were slain, and by your blood, you ransomed people for God from every tribe and language and people and nation, and you have made them a kingdom and priests to our God, and they shall reign on the earth." Then I looked, and I heard around the throne and the living creatures and the elders the voice of many angels, numbering myriads of myriads and thousands of thousands, saying with a loud voice, "Worthy is the Lamb who was slain, to receive power and wealth and wisdom and might and honor and glory and blessing!" (Revelation 5:6-12 NKJV)

All of the writers of the New Testament see the cross of Jesus as the purpose of all history. There are many great and wonderful events in history, but none of them equal the cross of Jesus. There have been scientific and medical discoveries that have changed and defeated certain diseases. There have been explorations into space and the discovery of just how big and wonderful this creation is. Wonderful inventions have been created to help amputees be able to walk. History is filled with great inventions that help make lives a little easier. As great as these inventions and discoveries are, they are nothing in comparison to the cross of Jesus.

The cross reveals just how great the love of God is for us.

The cross reveals just how terrible sin is.

The cross reveals the target and the purpose of sin. Yes, it is true that sin wants to destroy our lives, but the ultimate purpose of sin is to attack the heart of God. The purpose of sin is to weaken the power and the authority of God over his creation.

The cross reveals the seriousness of our crimes and the justice of our punishment.

Let's first consider the seriousness of our sins. This is one of those areas where many have difficulty with. They don't want to think of themselves as bad people. They compare themselves to others that they see or read about. They hear about men and women who commit terrible crimes such as human trafficking, selling highly addictive drugs, drunkenness, and theft. When we compare ourselves to others, we are always going to find someone who is worse than we are in our behavior. We are always going to see people who do more kinds of terrible things than we do. It is true that they may lie, lose their temper on occasion, or use profanity sometimes, but their sins do not seem to be as bad as others who commit serious crimes. We are not nearly as bad as the person who commits murder, molests children, or commits acts of terrorism. These people are much worse than us.

We have to agree that many sins are worse than other sins. Getting angry and losing our temper is not nearly as bad as a person who is involved in the sex trafficking of minors. Being jealous of another person's success is not as bad as someone assaulting another person.

The mistake we make when we compare our sins to others is that we forget or overlook what our sin, no matter how small or insignificant, does. In the context of the cross of Jesus, there are no small sins and big sins. Every sin caused the death of Jesus on the cross. The times we lied, those times we became angry or lashed out at someone because we were offended, causing the same kind of pain and suffering for Jesus on the cross as the sins of murder or terrorism. The Bible is very clear concerning sin. All sin is an attack on God. All sin is disobedience and rebellion against Him. All sin violates the law of God and, therefore, deserves punishment.

Psalms 51 says **Have mercy on me, O God, according to your steadfast love; according to your abundant mercy, blot out my transgressions. Wash me thoroughly from my iniquity, and cleanse me from my sin! For I know my transgressions and my sin is ever before me. Against you, you only, have I sinned and done what is evil in your sight so that you may be justified in your words and blameless in your judgment. (Psalms 51:1-4 NKJV)**

I said, "Lord be merciful to me; heal my soul, for I have sinned against you. (Psalm 51:4. NKJV)

What do these passages mean when they say, "We have sinned against God." The writer of the Psalms uses this language because he wants us to see just how serious our sin is. We are not just breaking some rule or manmade law. We are being disobedient to the creator of the universe. We are rebelling against His Word and

His commands. Most of all, we are causing pain and suffering to Jesus on the cross.

All of our sins are responsible for the nails in his hands and feet. What we consider to be little or insignificant sins are responsible for the crown of thorns crushed down on his head and the spear in his side. It was our sin that was responsible for the scourging and the beating He received before he died on that cross. This is how bad our sins are.

Considering that the one dying on the cross was the God-Man, then we realize that our sins were causing not just pain to Jesus but His death also. What, then, should be the punishment for sins against God? We understand that certain crimes carry different punishments in our society. For instance, if I threaten a neighbor or some other person, I will be investigated and could face a fine or some other kind of penalty. But if I threaten the President of the United States, I am going to get a serious visit from the Secret Service or FBI. Why is that? It is because of who is being threatened. The threat is the same, but the individual is different. The threat against the president carries greater consequences than the threat against a neighbor.

What, then, should the consequences be for sins against God? In our justice system, we say that punishment should fit the crime. A person who gets stopped for speeding is going to have a different consequence than a person who robs a jewelry store. Some punishments may require some community service time or a financial penalty. But if there are crimes against God, then the punishment for those crimes should be the most severe, and they are. Crimes and sins against God require one payment: an eternity of separation from God. There is no other penalty we can pay. We cannot do anything that puts us in the right relationship with God. The only thing we can do in our life when we sin is to commit more sin. We cannot stop.

The wonder and the great mystery of the coming of Jesus is that He came so we would not have to pay the penalty for our sins. He came to pay the price for our sins so we would not have to. It is amazing to consider that we who deserved eternal death have been offered eternal life because Jesus took our place in receiving the punishment for our sins.

The payment for our sin was to experience the wrath of God. If Jesus had not come, you and I would experience the fullness of the wrath of God on our sinfulness. The fullness of God's wrath is an eternity in hell. That is what we deserve. However, in some mysterious, wonderful, supernatural way, Jesus experienced the full wrath of God when he took our place on the cross. The Bible teaches that the suffering of Jesus was much more than just nails, a crown of thorns and a spear in the side. It was much more than a scourging and whipping. As horrible as all of these punishments were, the most excruciating punishment was when all of God's wrath and judgment were poured out on Jesus when He was on the cross. No part of His wrath was withheld. Jesus experienced it all. This is the cost of sinning against God. Jesus paid this cost, and we cannot experience an eternal relationship with God because they have all been paid for.

The cross shows the condition of all men and, at the same time, the hope for all men.

And you were dead in the trespasses and sins in which you once walked, following the course of this world, following the prince of the power of the air, the spirit that is now at work in the sons of disobedience—among whom we all once lived in the passions of our flesh, carrying out the desires of the body and the mind, and were by nature children of wrath, like the rest of mankind. But God, being rich in mercy, because of the great love with which he loved us, even when we were dead in our trespasses, made us alive together with Christ—by grace, you have been saved—and raised us up with him and seated us with him in the heavenly places in Christ Jesus so that in the coming ages he might show the immeasurable riches of his grace in kindness toward us in Christ Jesus. (Ephesians 2:1-7. ESV)

What a terrible condition we were in:

We were Dead in sin.

Headed in the wrong direction in the world. The direction away from God.

We're driven by the sinful passions of the flesh.

We deserved the wrath of God.

This was our spiritual condition. We were deserving of eternal death. But we have been radically changed because Jesus died on the cross for us. We did not deserve any grace or mercy from God. Thankfully, God did not give us what we deserved. He gave us the grace of salvation. All of this grace, compassion, and salvation came about because of the glory of the cross.

Chapter 12
The Glory of His Resurrection

Until Christ came to this world, God was hidden from men. Man could not have an intimate relationship with Him. Karl Barth stated that the reason men could not have any kind of intimate relationship with God was because God was other that His creation. What he meant by that was that God was so different from men that it was impossible for us to know Him intimately and even have a relationship with Him. Jesus spoke of the "Otherness of God" when He said God is Spirit and those who worship Him must worship Him in Spirit and in truth. (John 4:24. ESV).

Even when Jesus came, God was still hidden. What I mean by that is that when men and women looked at Jesus, they saw a man. They did not see someone who looked like an artist rendering of Jesus with a halo around his head. They saw an ordinary man. They knew where He was born. They knew His parents and family. Because of the humanness of Jesus, people just could not believe that He was God in the flesh. When He made the claim that He was the Messiah, His hearers became so angry they wanted to throw Him off of a cliff and kill Him. They could not believe He was nothing more than a man. They refused to believe that He was the Messiah.

Even though they did not recognize Him as God in the flesh, they did recognize that God was with Him in a special way. Nicodemus came to Jesus and said, We know you are from God because no one can do these things except God be with Him. (John 3:2). In the minds of those who heard Him and watched Him, they were convinced not that He was the Son of God but that He was like one of the prophets in the Old Testament. On one occasion, Jesus asked His disciples who people thought He was. Some thought He was Jeremiah. Others said that He was John the Baptist raised from the dead. None of them thought that He was the Son of God.

The resurrection proves that Jesus is who He said He is.

The Old Testament tells of the coming of the Messiah. It describes the work He would do in redeeming the world from sin.

Several commentators describe the Old Testament as the testament of expectation. This expectation was fulfilled when Jesus was born in Bethlehem. The greatest expectation was the bringing forth the Kingdom of God. God's expectation in sending His son into the world was to reconcile men and women to Himself. He wanted to adopt us as His children, but He could not do that until He died for sin and then was resurrected.

If Jesus was not raised from the dead, then the cross would be nothing more than the execution of a criminal who deserved to die. If Jesus had not been raised from the dead, then there would be no salvation, and it would have been proven that Jesus was a liar when the resurrection of Jesus had two proofs.

Our Sin is paid for.

The one who paid the price for our sin was God Himself.

All of the writers of the New Testament speak about who Jesus is. They write that he is God who became a man. They write with confidence and without hesitation. They have no doubt who Jesus is because of the resurrection. They watched Him die. Some of them took His body down from the cross and buried Him. Three days later, He appeared to them as the resurrected Lord. After the resurrection, Jesus spent forty days with them, teaching them and doing other works.

They then watched Him ascend into heaven. They had no doubt that this same Jesus who was crucified was the same Jesus who rose from the dead. They ate with Him, touched Him, talked with Him.

Luke describes the conversation that two of His disciples had with Him after the resurrection. This risen Lord took the time to show them how all of the Old Testament talked about the Messiah: how He would be crucified and then how He would be raised from the dead. After spending time walking and talking with Him, they invited Him to have a meal with them. Luke says **When he was at table with them, he took the bread and blessed and broke it and gave it to them. And their eyes were opened, and they recognized him. And he vanished from their sight. (Luke 24:30-31 ESV).** They knew without a doubt that He was the same Jesus who was crucified, and now HE WAS ALIVE.

The resurrection is the event that reveals God.

Up until that time, God was hidden from men. That is, the fullness of His glory was hidden. Until the resurrection, people would assume that Jesus was nothing more than a prophet or a miracle worker. He would have been considered a good, moral, and ethical man. With the resurrection, we can now see Jesus as God.

To the Hindus, Jesus was a man who realized God's consciousness and showed that if everyone worked hard, they could realize God's consciousness also. They believe that God's consciousness, Christ's consciousness, Krishna's consciousness, and Buddha's consciousness are all the same thing. This means, in their theology, that Jesus was just a great religious teacher among other great religious teachers.

Hari Krishnas believe that Krishna and Jesus are the same person. In their theology, it really does not matter what you believe as long as you believe in God. It does not matter what God you believe in.

Note that none of these religions accept the revelation that God became a man, died on the cross, and then rose from the dead.

The writers of the New Testament were willing to die for the message that said Jesus was God in the flesh, who died on a cross and then rose from the dead. None of them were willing to refute that. The early Christians had this same commitment to this belief. They were willing to die, confessing that Jesus was God and He was the only way to everlasting life.

The very nature of these disciples changed because of the resurrection. These men who were once afraid of everything became fearless and unafraid to share the gospel of the risen Lord. They knew that no matter what happened to them, even if they died, they would be raised from the dead in the same way that Jesus was raised. Because of the resurrection, they knew there was nothing that could happen to them that God could not overcome, even death. After all, if He can overcome death, then He can overcome anything.

Acts 5 describes the time when Peter and John were brought before the religious leaders and told not to teach in Jesus' name. Look at the courage of these apostles as they answered these men.

Then, they brought the apostles in before the council. Didn't we tell you never again to teach in this man's name?" the high priest demanded. Instead, you have filled all Jerusalem with your teachings about Jesus, and you intend to blame us for His death." But Peter and the apostles replied, "We must obey God rather than human authority. The God of our ancestors raised Jesus from the dead after you killed him by crucifying him. Then God put him in the place of honor at his right hand as Prince and Savior. He did this to give the people of Israel an opportunity to turn from their sins and turn to God so their sins would be forgiven. We are witnesses of these things and so is the Holy Spirit who is given by God to those who obey Him. (Acts 5:27-32 NLT)

Did you notice the boldness of the apostles in this passage? This is the same apostle, Peter, who denied the Lord three times on the night of His trial. These were the same apostles who ran away and hid in fear that they would be executed for being followers of Jesus. These were the same men who hid in a closed room all weekend as Jesus was in the grave. Now, they are different. What was the difference? Peter says that difference is because of what they witnessed. He told these religious leaders, We are witnesses of these things. What things? They were witnesses of the resurrection of Jesus. They saw Him alive and spent time with Him before He ascended into heaven. They were witness to the coming of the Holy Spirit, who descended on them in tongues of fire on the day of Pentecost. They were witnesses to thousands of people whose lives were changed because they believed in the truth of God. Because they were witnesses of these events, there was nothing they were afraid of. They were filled with boldness because Jesus rose from the dead.

The meaning of the resurrection for those who believe.

When Jesus rose from the dead, everything became new. He had a new body, a glorified body. He rose to new experiences where he would never suffer again. He rose to a place of exaltation above every name and person. These men knew that Jesus was now seated at the right hand of the Father in heaven. He is in a position of utmost authority and power.

The resurrection means that everything becomes new for the believer.

2 Corinthians 5:17

What this means is that those who become Christians become new persons. They are not the same anymore, for the old life is gone. A new life has begun. (NLT)

Romans 6:4-8

For we died and were buried with Christ by baptism. And just as Christ was raised from the dead by the glorious power of the Father, now we also may live new lives. Since we have been united with him in his death, we will also be raised as he was. Our old sinful selves were crucified with Christ so that sin might lose its power in our lives. We are no longer slaves to sin. For when we died with Christ, we were set free from the power of sin. And since we died with

Christ, we know we will also share his new life.

Because of the resurrection of Jesus, **the grave has a different meaning for believers.** It is not the ending point of our life but a transition. In the Old Testament, the grave was dark and had a sense of hopelessness, but for the Christian, this hopelessness is replaced with hope and assurance. We have this hope because Jesus rose from the dead and promised that if we believe in Him, we, too, shall rise from the dead.

Because of the resurrection, the New Testament is a message of glad tidings of great joy. It is truly good news for all who believe. The person who accepts this good news for himself suddenly finds that the burden of paying for our sins has been taken away. His debt has been paid on the cross, and the resurrection shows that God has accepted that payment. The believer no longer has been set free from the debt he owed. Not only has our debt been paid for, but we no longer have to be overcome by the sin we were indebted to. We have been set free from the debt and the power of sin because of the resurrection of Jesus.

The fear of death is removed from the believer. Death has lost its power because the believer knows that something better awaits him. This was never more evident to me as a pastor when I visited a church member who had a terminal illness and was close to death. During his illness, he and I had many conversations about heaven and about what it meant to die. He asked a lot of questions. He wondered what Jesus looked like. He asked about heaven and seeing loved ones. As the time for his death came closer, he became more calm and actually was anticipating dying. He was actually looking forward to seeing Jesus and going to heaven.

One of the most remarkable conversations we had was our last. He was sitting on the couch next to his wife and was talking openly about what he was looking forward to. He then made a statement I never heard anyone else say. He said, "Brother Ronnie, If I don't die, I am going to be disappointed." What a statement.

Another dear friend of mine was dying from a long-term illness. He was tired from the sickness and the suffering from all the medicines he was taking. He told me in one of our last visits, "Brother Ronnie, I'm ready to go home." It was not long before the Lord honored his wish and brought him home.

These men and others like them came to the end of their lives without any fear. They knew that because Jesus rose from the dead, they, too, would be with Him in heaven.

Because of the resurrection, **suffering takes on a new meaning**. The Christian knows that he will experience suffering in this world because Jesus suffered. Jesus said **you will have tribulation because I had tribulation. You will be hated because I was hated.** The Christian also knows something else that is of greater importance. We may go through severe suffering, persecution, and tribulation while here on earth, but there is no comparison to the joy we will experience in heaven. The suffering in this world cannot compare to the glory that awaits us, in particular, the glory of being in the presence of Jesus for eternity.

The resurrection removes us as the objects of God's wrath.
God poured out his wrath on His son as he hung on the cross. The wrath of God was poured out for all the sins of all mankind. The resurrection shows that the full wrath of God is emptied. There is nothing left for God to pour out. When Jesus said **It is finished** He was saying that the work He came to do is finished. He was also saying that the cup of God's wrath is empty. It is like drinking a glass of water. When the last drop is gone, we put the glass down and say finished. God's wrath is finished, and those who believe in Jesus as their savior will never experience it. We will only experience grace, salvation, and being in his eternal presence.

THE RESURRECTION INDICATES THAT GOD IS PRESENT AND GOD IS COMING.

As was stated earlier, the Old Testament was the testament of expectation. It was proclaiming the coming of the Messiah. The New Testament is the witness of recollection. It is the witness that Christ has come. Not only has Christ come, but He is also present. Before Jesus ascended back to heaven, He told His disciples, **Behold, I am with you even unto the end of the age. (Matthew 28:20)**. This means that there is never a moment that we are out of His presence. This presence is a spiritual presence, but it is a very real presence.

The birth and the existence of the church are evidence of His presence. The New Testament identifies the church in different ways. First, the church is identified as the **bride of Christ**. Second, the church is identified as **the body of Christ**. Finally, the church is identified as **His temple**. Each of these identities expresses the presence of Jesus with His people. He is the Husband who is always present and attentive to the needs of HIs bride. When we opened our hearts to believe in Him, He moved into us. His spirit indwells all of those who believe in Him. His presence in us is an eternal presence. He will never leave us under any circumstances.

We experience the presence of Christ when He performs miracles. Every time we pray for those who are sick, and they experience healing, that is an indication of His presence. This means that he was near us to hear us and then answer us.

We experience His presence when we spend time in prayer. Jesus said, **when two or three are gathered in my name, there I am in the midst of them. (Matthew 18:20)** When we combine our prayer time with reading, studying, and meditating on the Word, we experience His presence. Jesus told His disciples that He needed to go away so that the Holy Spirit could come and indwell us. When the Holy Spirit comes to live in us, He becomes our teacher of the Word we study.

We experience His presence when we gather to worship. The Psalms says that the Lord inhabits the praise of His people. Every time we come together as a church to worship, the Lord is present. He is present when we sing, pray, listen to a sermon, and fellowship with other believers.

One of my favorite songs was written by Phillips, Craig, and Dean. The title is His Favorite Song of All.

He loves to hear the wind sing

As it whistles through the pines on mountain peeks

And He loves to hear the raindrops

As they splash to the ground in a magic melody

He smiles in sweet approval

As the waves crash through the rocks in harmony

And creation joins in unity

To sing to Him majestic symphonies

But His favorite song of all

Is the song of the Redeemed

When lost sinners, now made clean

Lift their voices, loud and strong

When those purchased by His blood

Lift to Him a song of love

There's nothin' more He'd rather hear

Nor so pleasin' to His ear

As His favorite song of all

And He loves to hear the angels

As they sing, "Holy, holy is the Lamb"

Heaven's choirs in harmony

Lift up praises to the Great I Am

But He lifts His hands for silence

When the weakest, saved by grace, begins to sing

And a million angels listen

As a newborn soul sings, "I've been redeemed"

Cause His favorite song of all

Is the song of the redeemed

When lost sinners, now made clean

Lift their voices, loud and strong

When those purchased by His blood

Lift to Him a song of love

There's nothin' more He'd rather hear

Nor so pleasin' to His ear

As His favorite song of all

It's not just melodies and harmonies

That catches His attention

It's not just clever lines and phrases

That causes Him to stop and listen

But when any heart set free

Washed and bought by Calvary, begins to sing

That's His favorite song of all

Is the song of the redeemed

When lost sinners, now made clean

Lift their voices, loud and strong

When those purchased by His blood

Lift to Him a song of love

There's nothin' more He'd rather hear

Nor so pleasin' to His ear

As His favorite song of all

Holy, holy, holy is the Lamb

Halleluiah, halleluiah.

(Favorite Song of All lyrics © Capitol CMG Publishing)

I love these lyrics because I believe them to be true. We can look around and see all the beauty of creation. Each of us have sounds of nature that are pleasant to us. I, for one, love to hear the sound of rain falling. It is so relaxing. It makes me want to rest and sleep. I love to hear the breeze as it gently blows through the trees of my yard. As pleasant as all these sounds are, the one that gets the attention of God more than any other is the sound of His people singing praises to Him. It is the sound of one of His children calling out to Him and expressing joy and praise for who He is. These songs and prayers are His favorite.

Not only is our Lord present, but He is coming again.

Jesus said that He was going to return one day. He said, **In a day and hour that you least expected it, the son of man will come again. (Matthew 24:44).** From the moment that Jesus ascended into heaven, the disciples were looking forward to His return. They thought that He would return soon, but He told them that His coming would be at an unexpected time. But it is a time known only to the Father.

This coming of the Lord is something every believer should look forward to with joy and anticipation. It is good news that the Lord is not going to leave us in a world that is deteriorating day by day. Each of us knows what it means to wait in anticipation for some good news or for some upcoming event. A doctor comes out of surgery with the good news that a tumor is not malignant. A new father comes out of the delivery room holding his newborn baby and has good news that he is healthy. Can you imagine the utter joy that must have come to these writers of the New Testament knowing that this resurrected Lord was going to return? Each of them hoped that He would come in their lifetime.

This should be the attitude of every believer. We should get up every day with the expectation that this could be the day when our Lord returns to take us home. As one preacher shared in a sermon outline:

He has come.

He is here.

He is coming.

Finally, because of the resurrection, we live with the knowledge that Jesus is working in our lives to make us like him.

The resurrection of Jesus gives God the opportunity to transform us into the likeness of His son. From the moment we accept Jesus as our savior, God began a work in us. That work was to make us more like Jesus. He is transforming us into the image of Jesus. This transforming process will continue until we die or until the Lord returns. Every day, we can get up with the expectation and the anticipation that God is going to do something in us, for us or to us, that will make us more like Jesus. Making us like Jesus may not always be a pleasant experience. Some of us may have the same kind of experience as Job. We may go through some dark times, but it helps to remember that those dark times are not God punishing us but God molding us. He is shaping us to be more like Jesus.

None of this would be possible if there had not been a resurrection. It was a glorious, powerful morning when the angel came down and rolled the stone away from the tomb. He did not do this so Jesus could get out, but He did this so we could see in. We could see that the tomb was empty. He is Risen. He is Risen, indeed. What a glorious moment. And we get to experience the resurrected Lord every day.

Chapter 13
The Glory That Lives In Us

There is so much wonder in our salvation that it is difficult to explore them all. In this study, we have focused on how God wants us to know Him. He knew that it was impossible for us to know anything about Him. We stated earlier that when we try to conceive of God in our natural minds, we come up with all kinds of depraved theologies, cults, and religions. This is why there is so much idolatry in the world. It is because men have been trying to make God in their own image or the image we think God is. All of these attempts to find God and know God in our own intellectual ability are futile. God, therefore, reveals Himself to us so we can know Him and have an understanding of Him. This is where the work of the Holy Spirit comes in.

The first work of the Holy Spirit in our lives is to bring conviction of sin.

In John 16:8, Jesus describes the work of the Holy Spirit in regard to sin. **And when He comes, He will convict the world in regard to sin and righteousness and judgment. Of sin, because they do not believe in me…(NKJV).** Jesus told His disciples that He needed to go away so the Holy Spirit could come. The Holy Spirit was needed to do what Jesus could not do in a physical body. In His body, Jesus could, like us, be in one place at a time. He was limited in His ability to be present in everyone. When the Holy Spirit came, He was not limited to physicality. He is able to be all over the world at one time. He can speak to people in remote areas of the world while, at the same time, empowering the sharing of the gospel everywhere.

Notice Jesus said in this verse that **the Holy Spirit will convict the World of sin.** How does He do that? He does it through the witness of His disciples. The Bible says in Acts 2 that the Holy Spirit came in tongues of fire and entered into the disciples who were in the upper room. A few moments later, after Peter preached a sermon, 3000 people were saved. The people who were saved were from all over the world. **Astounded and amazed, they asked,**

"Are not all these men speaking Galileans? How is it them that each of us hears them in his own native language? Parthians, Medes, Elamites, residents of Mesopotamia, Jude's and Cappadocia, Pontus, and Asia. (Acts 2:7-9. NKJV).

Once these men and women heard the gospel, the Bible says that they were convicted of their sin and their needs. In verse 37, the Bible says, And when they heard this, they were cut to the heart and said to Peter and the other apostles, **"Brothers, what shall we do? (NIV)**

Other translations give a different expression of what happened to those who heard the presentation from Peter. Here are some of them.

Peters words pierced their hearts…(NLT)

When they heard this they were pricked in their heart…(KJV)

When they heard this, they came under deep conviction… (Holman Christian Standard Bible)

When they heard these things, They were stricken in their hearts (Aramaic Bible in Plain English)

Each of these translations uses different words to express the same emotion. Those who heard the message of Jesus' death and resurrection were convicted of their need. According to Jesus, this conviction comes from the Holy Spirit. When they heard the gospel, they saw their need. They saw their guilt and felt condemnation. This came from the Holy Spirit applying the word of God to their hearts. These men and women would have never experienced this conviction if it were not for the work of the Holy Spirit. They would not have been saved if they had not been convicted by the Holy Spirit.

After the days of Pentecost were over, all of those men and women who were convicted of their sins eventually returned to the country they were from. Since the Holy Spirit now lived in these new believers, He went with them to various places around the world. As these men and women shared their testimony about their faith in

Jesus, the Holy Spirit was able to take their testimony and bring conviction to those who were hearing the gospel.

He did the same work through the apostles as they also went to various places in the world to preach and teach about Jesus. These men could not be everywhere, but as the Holy Spirit moved into the lives of these new believers, He was able to work everywhere.

I love reading about the revivals and awakenings that took place in history around the world. In each of the revivals and awakenings, the work of the Holy Spirit in bringing conviction is evident. It is reported that when Jonathan Edwards preached his famous sermon Sinners in the Hands of an Angry God, he was not able to finish because of the impact it was having on the congregation. While He was preaching, people listening shrieked and cried out, and the crying and weeping became so loud that he could not continue. Instead, he went down among the people and prayed with them in groups. Many came to a saving knowledge of Christ that day. **(This Day in History: Jonathan Edwards preaches "Sinners in the hands of an angry God." Article by Jess Edwards, July 8, 2018).** This outcry came from the conviction of the Holy Spirit.

The work of the Holy Spirit in the Second Great Awakening is recorded throughout America. According to Phil Ryken, the work of the Holy Spirit spread through the preaching of the gospel by various ministers in different locations. It is recorded that George Whitfield preached the gospel to tens of thousands in Philadelphia. Down in Virginia, by the providence of God, a slaveholder found a few pages torn from Thomas Boston's wonderful book The Fourfold State of Man. Not only was the man converted, but a revival broke out among his slaves. **(The Great Awakening; 1725-1760, Phil Ryken, October 24, 1999)**

The point here is that the Holy Spirit is able to work through all of the world through the witness of believers in Jesus. This is the reason Jesus said that **He needed to go away so the Holy Spirit could come.** If there is no conviction, then no one can be saved. There can be no conversion simply because we chose to be converted. We choose to be converted when we are first convicted by the Spirit.

After the Holy Spirit brings conviction for sin, He then gives us the ability to understand the Word of God. Once that is given, the Holy Spirit then gives us the faith to believe. **For by grace, you have been saved through faith. And this is not of your own doing, it is a gift of God. (Ephesians 2:8 ESV).** Paul makes it clear in the Ephesians letter that our salvation did not come about because of anything we did. It came about because of everything the Holy Spirit did. He first convicted us and then gave us the ability to believe. Faith to believe is His gift to us.

Once we exercise this gift of faith to believe in Jesus as savior, the Holy Spirit then does the work of cleansing, washing and entering. **He saved us not because of righteous things we had done but because of His mercy. He washed away our sins, giving us a new birth and new life through the Holy Spirit. (Titus 3:5 NLT)** Everything about our salvation comes from the Holy Spirit. He convicted us, washed us, cleansed us from sin, and gave us the gift of faith.

After using the faith given to us to believe, the Holy Spirit then moved into us. I Corinthians 6:19 **says do you not know that your body is a temple of the Holy Spirit within you, whom you have from God? You are not your own, You are bought with a price. Therefore, glorify God in your body. (NKJV).** This is really an incredible passage of scripture. The Holy Spirit moves in us at conversion. He remains with us to help us and guide us in our Christian growth.

The glory of the living God now lives inside of us. Let's consider what He does in our lives.

The Holy Spirit gives us spiritual fruit such as love, joy and patience. **But the fruit of the Spirit is love, joy, peace, forbearance, kindness, goodness, faithfulness…(Galatians 5:22)**

The Holy Spirit teaches us. When we read the Word of God, the Holy Spirit illuminates the scripture for us. **And we Impart this in words not taught by human wisdom but taught by the Spirit, interpreting spiritual truths to those who are spiritual (Corinthians 2:13 ESV)**

The Holy Spirit prays for us when we don't know what to pray for or are unable to express what we want to. **Likewise, the Spirit helps us with our weaknesses. For we do not know what to pray as we ought, but the Holy Spirit prays for us with groaning that cannot be expressed in words. (Romans 8;26 ESV)**

This is not an exhaustive list of what the Spirit does with us and in us, but these are examples of how the Spirit works in our lives. All of this teaching, praying and empowering is for one primary purpose, and that is so He can glorify God in our bodies. He also wants to exalt and lift up Jesus so others can be saved.

What a wonderful experience. The Holy Spirit lives in us. The Holy Spirit is also known as the Spirit of Christ. He lives inside of our bodies to bless us, strengthen us, fill us and teach us. This glory is in us. Our prayer should always be that others can see the glory of Jesus in us.

THE HOLY SPIRIT EXPRESSES THE LOVE OF GOD THROUGH US

God's desire has always been to reveal Himself to the world. The fullness of His revelation was fulfilled with the coming of Jesus. Through His comings, we can know God in ways that we could never know Him before. Jesus has now ascended into heaven for the purpose of being able to reveal God through his new earthly body which is the church. As we stated earlier, while Jesus was here, in the flesh, He was limited in that He could be only in one place at a time. Now, in his church, He can reveal Himself all over the world.

The way God reveals Himself through His church is the same way He revealed Himself through Jesus. Jesus said that **He came to do the will of the Father. He said He does those things that He sees His Father doing.** So, the first way that Jesus revealed the Father was through the things that He did. He healed the sick, raised the dead, taught about and defined the Kingdom of God and performed many different kinds of miracles. Through His work, he revealed that He had power and authority over sickness, disease, demons and devils, nature and even death.

The second way that Jesus revealed the Father, and most likely the greatest way, was by loving people. Most people, when they thought of God, thought of Him as wrathful and angry. Even though many scriptures in the Old Testament talked of God as being merciful, compassionate and forgiving, many lived under the fear that if they did not follow all of the rules and traditions that were taught by the religious leaders, they would be condemned by God. They feared that if they did not offer an unblemished sacrifice, God would not accept it. Jesus came to show them that God was a God of Love. Yes, he condemned sin and unrighteousness, but He loved His creation. He loved Israel, and He loved the Gentile world.

Jesus spent His entire ministry expressing the love of God to everyone He came in contact with. He loved them because the people were **like sheep without a shepherd**. He told His disciples that He would love them till the end of time. John refers to this love in his letter when he says, **Behold what manner of love the Father has bestowed on. Us that we should be called the children of God.** The love of God revealed through Jesus is the greatest revelation in all of history. God loves us even though we are nothing in comparison to all of His creation. He loved us even when we failed. He loved us when we were rebellious and sinful against Him.

God continues to reveal this love through His church: you and me. The church reveals the love of God by living out what He says in His word. One preacher said that the world can see the love of God when believers do the word. What did He mean by that statement? It means that when Christians do what God says in His word and when we live in obedience to Him, the world sees the joy and peace we have because of that obedience to Him. The second way God reveals Himself through us is when we love one another and love others who are not a part of the church.

Loving as God loves

The New Testament teaches that when a person becomes a believer, there is a radical change in his life. He becomes different in everything. Paul that that when we become a believer, we become a **new creation; old things have passed away, and all things become new.** One of the new characteristics of this new life is the way we love. We love like God loves. We express the love of God in our actions and attitudes toward others. If the expression of the love of God does not flow through us, then it could be a sign that we do not have a relationship with God. A relationship with God changes us, but if we are acting the same way as we did before we professed Christ, it could be a sign that we really do not know Him. Love is the natural outcome of faith in Jesus.

Love is the evidence of faith

Galatians 5:5-6 says, "Be we who live by the Spirit eagerly wait to receive everything promised to us who are right with God through faith. For when we place our faith in Jesus Christ, it make no difference to God whether we are circumcised or not. What is important is FAITH EXPRESSING ITSELF IN LOVE. (NLT)

Some members of the Galatian church were taught that faith in Christ was noted as all that was needed for salvation. They were being told by false teachers that they needed Christ as a savior, but they also needed the law as well. Paul writes and informs them that Christ set them free from the law when they received His new life. The new life came about because of faith alone. Paul also taught not only the Galatian church but all of the other churches that he wrote to that Christ set all believers free from the curse of the law. Even though Jesus set them free from the punishment and condemnation of the law, there were other visible results that proved their relationship to Jesus.

The first result is that those who have Christ as their savior also have an unquenchable desire to know as much about Him as possible. He reminds them that God has so much more for them than just being saved. There is a life to live: a life of faith, victory, witness, struggle, learning, growing, praising, witnessing, testifying and worship. This means that there is never a time when our life is empty. A Christian who is living out his faith in Christ cannot say that he or she is bored. They can't say that they don't have anything to do because their day is filled with all kinds of activities to grow spiritually.

We are to work at our jobs with the attitude that we are working for Jesus, and we want to do our best for Him.

We are to be faithful in our praise and worship.

We are to be reading, learning and meditating on the Word of God.

We are to constantly be aware of His presence with us and in us.

Because of the presence of the Holy Spirit in us, our entire life is lived in that presence. There is never a moment we are outside of His presence or His care. His presence and love are so overwhelming that the only response we can have is to let this love flow from Him through us to the world around us. The question has been asked, "How can a heart embrace Him who is supreme love without glowing with love and love energy? If God is love, and He is, then His love is something that cannot be contained in us. We must express it. It becomes impossible to keep it to ourselves. **"(Lenski's New Testament Commentary—The interpretation of St Pauls Epistles to the Galatians, to the Ephesians and to the Philippians, Pg 262)**

Love proves that we know God

Dear friends, let us continue to love one another, for love comes from God. Anyone who loves is born of God and knows God. But anyone who does not love does not know God—-for God is love. (2 John 4:7-8 NLT)

John says that we cannot claim to have a knowledge of God if we do not love others. God dwells within the life of the believer. God is love. Therefore, the believer cannot help but love others.

Love is the revelation of God in us

No one has ever seen God. But if we love each other, God lives in us, and His love has been brought to full expression through us. (I John 4:12 NLT)

It is through this expression of love that the world can see God. Remember, the desire of God is to reveal Himself to the world. He wants to reveal His nature and character. His nature is love. His love is in us. When we express that love, then the world can see God. When we love others, God's will is being accomplished through us.

James said that **we must be doers of the word,** and the greatest doing of the word is loving others the same way God loves us. This expression of love is the essence of Christian living.

Love bears all things.

Love bears all things, believes all things, hopes all things and endures all things. (1 Corinthians 13:7. NKJV)

The 13th chapter of First Corinthians is one of the most popular and the most quoted in the Bible. It describes the purest and most Godly form and expression of love. In the verse above, Paul says that Love bears all things. The word used for bear is to describe the holding up of a heavy burden or the carrying of a heavyweight. It describes the ability to endure and quietly suffer through afflictions and difficulties. When tough times come, love does not complain and groans about how bad things are. Love has a great capacity for enduring suffering and trials.

The greatest example of this enduring love is found in the death of Jesus on the cross. Jesus bore our sins, shame and suffering on that cross. Jesus endured the most horrible kind of death imaginable. He patiently endured the wrath of God poured out on him. This wrath was not because of anything Jesus did, but it was for everything that we did. The wrath that we deserved was poured out on Jesus, who did not deserve it. He endured the wrath of God in our place. This is what Paul meant when he said, Love endured all things.

When Christians experience hardships in life and quietly endure them, doing their best to be an example of what it means to trust God and be faithful even when things are bad is love. The love of God in the life of the Christians has the ability to experience great suffering and still glorify God.

Love builds up the church.

Instead, we will hold to the truth in love, becoming more and more in every way like Christ, who is the head of His body, the church. Under His direction, the whole body is fitted together perfectly. As each part does its own special work, it helps the other parts grow, so that the whole body is healthy and growing and full of love. (Ephesians 4:15-16)

The members of the church are being fitted together. We can imagine a great puzzle with all the pieces separated and lying in a pile. Someone comes along and begins to fit those separate pieces together. As soon as more and more pieces are fitted together, the picture becomes clear. This is Paul's description of the church. God begins to fit all of those pieces together. He works to form us into His living body so He can reveal Himself to the world. This verse says that we are being fitted together under his direction and are being fitted together perfectly.

Paul does not only speak of the church being perfectly fitted together, but he speaks of a **healthy church**. A healthy church is not one that is just gifted. It is not a church that has strong personalities and a great program. No. A healthy church is one that is full of love. It is this continual expression of love that causes the church to grow and remain strong. It is this love that allows God to reveal Himself to the world.

It is love that accepts people from all walks of life. It is love that says come as you are, and you will be accepted. Our message to the world is not to come to church and be like us. No. The message of the church to the world is **to come as you are, and we will love you.** Come as you are, and we will reveal the nature of God to you.

The nature and love of God is seen in Jesus as he touches the lepers, forgives the prostitute, eats with notorious sinners and offers the worst of the worst an invitation to the Kingdom of God. When the church loves people of the world like this, it is revealing the nature and the person of G do. When we love like this, we are being the body of Christ.

None of these expressions of love are possible without the presence of the Holy Spirit. It is His presence that makes it possible for love to be expressed in the truest sense. This means that the love of God found in the life of the believer has nothing to do with sentiment, feelings or opinion. It has to do with being true to ourselves, people who have been radically changed through faith in Jesus.

We are radically changed through love.

If we have been radically changed through our faith in Christ, then the evidence of that change is our love for God. His love in us will produce continual action on our part. That action will be to continually seek Him for the purpose of knowing Him intimately. God revealed Himself to us. That revelation compels us to want to know more of Him. Paul expressed this same desire in Philippians.

But no, rather, I also count all things to be loss for the excellency of the knowledge of Christ Jesus my Lord, for whose sake I have suffered the loss of all things and count them as dung so that I may win Christ and be found in Him; to having my own righteousness, which is of the Law, but through faith in Christ, the righteousness of God by faith. That I may know Him and the power of His resurrection and the fellowship of His suffering, being made conformable to His death. (Philippians 3:89-10. MKJV). This radical change in us means we can't help but want to know more of Him. There is something in us that compels us to read, pray, study and meditate on the Word to know more of Him. This desire to know Him never leaves the believer. He finds joy in discovering something about Jesus that he did not know before.

This desire to know Him does not come naturally from within us. It comes supernaturally from the presence of the Holy Spirit. The Holy Spirit puts the desire to have an intimate relationship with God. This desire reveals a wonderful fact. It reveals that God can be and wants us to know Him. If God could not be known, if it were not possible to have an intimate relationship with Him, then the Holy Spirit would not have put this desire in us.

God expresses this possibility of knowing Him in the Old Testament.

When Israel was a child, I loved him as a son, and I called my son out of Egypt. But the more I called to him, the more he rebelled, offering sacrifices to the images of Baal and burning incense to idols. It was I who taught Israel how to walk, leading him along by the hand. But he doesn't know or even care that it was I who took care of him. I led Israel along with my ropes of kindness and love. I lifted the yoke from his neck, and I myself stooped to feed him. (Hosea 4:1-4 NLT)

Notice the intimacy of these verses. He loved Israel like a son. He taught him to walk by holding his hand. He led him with ropes of love and kindness. He took the burden of slavery from them. All of this passage describes closeness and intimacy, but the saddest part of this passage is that Israel didn't know any of this. They removed the memory of God's deliverance, care and goodness from their minds. Now, they were focused on false gods. They were living in rebellion. We can only imagine the heart of God as the people He loved did not know Him. They rejected this intimacy with God.

Jeremiah 31:3 says: Long ago the Lord said to Israel; "I have loved you my people with an everlasting love. With unfailing love, I have drawn you to myself. (NLT). The Lord speaks through Jeremiah of an everlasting love: an unfailing love. With this love, He draws them to Himself. It is a picture of a parent taking a child and holding that child close to His heart. I, as a parent, have done that very thing with my children and grandchildren. Most of us who have children know the reality of this as we hold our children close and love them because they are our children. To draw them close refers to intimacy.

In the New Testament, Jesus describes Himself as **the door.** This door leads to eternal life. This door also leads to a knowledge of God and of His love. Jesus describes the love of God in various ways.

It is the Love of a friend

This is my commandment that you love one another as I have loved you. Greater love has not one than this, than to lay down ones life for his friends. You are my friends if you do whatever I command you. (John 15;12-14. NKJV)

It is the love of a father for His children

Behold what manner of love the Father has bestowed on us that we should be called the children of God! (1 John 3:2)

The closer and more intimate we become with God, the more amazed we become at His love for us. It is a love that is indescribable. We do not have enough words in our vocabulary to describe the love that God has for us. At the same time, the more that we learn of his love for us, even though we can't adequately describe it, the more we love Him.

His love is the love of self-sacrifice

Remember, when we speak of self-sacrifice, we are speaking of the self-sacrifice of God for us. He comes into our existence and into our time. By coming into our world, He sends a message that is incredible. He is saying, **I am with you, and I am for you.** He reveals that He is aware of everything about our lives. He knows about all of our circumstances. He knows the struggles we are having, the trials we are going through, the temptations that attack us. By His coming, He also reveals that He is **available to us**. He is here with us right now. Because He is here with us, we do not have to be afraid of anything.

He comes to us for the purpose of claiming our shame and our guilt. He accepts the curse that was meant for us. Because He took upon Himself our shame, guilt and sin, we can be presented to God as **spotless and pure**. That is an incredible statement. We, who are sinners, covered with the filth and the stench of our sin, are now clean and pure. We are able to go into the presence of God, not as dirty, filthy sinners but as children made pure and clean through the work of the Spirit in us. All of this was not because we deserved it. All of this was because He loved us.

Because of this love given to us, we can boldly declare that we **are more than conquerors through Him who loved us (Romans 8:37).** In the context of this [passage, Paul is saying that it does not matter what circumstances we face. We can rise above them, endure them and have victory over them. Why? It is because God loves us. No matter what we experience in our life, the good or the bad, there is one great truth. **God loves me**, and that love for me never changes.

To adequately describe the Love of God, we simply say Jesus.

It is here in the person of Jesus that God meets us and draws us to Himself. This is what John meant when he said, **we love Him because He first loved us.** He came to us first. He first sacrificed Himself for us. He paid the price for our sins on the cross. He gave us an invitation to enter into His kingdom. How do we not love Him back? How do we not love others? It is this Love that has radically changed us. **We must love Him**.

When we examine the details of God's love for us and the sacrifice He made for us, we can now understand more clearly the first command given by God. **Here o Israel, the Lord your God is one. You shall love the Lord your God with all of your heart, all of your soul and all your strength. (Deuteronomy 6:4-5)**

Notice the number of times the command says "all". We are to love Him with all of our being. He loved us with the totality of His being. He loved us long before we were born. He loved us by planning to save us from our sins long before we were alive. He fulfilled that plan by sending Jesus to die on the cross to save us from our sins. Because He loved us like that, it is unreasonable for us not to love Him with our whole being. To not love Him with everything we are is to mock His love for us. It is to cheapen the act of His love demonstrated through Jesus.

The command to love God is given to His people.

In conclusion, it needs to be noted that this command was not given to the world in general. It was not given to all humanity. It was given to the people of God. The command speaks of **God being your God.** It is given to the people of God because only the people of God can fulfil this command. The rest of the world does not have the capacity to love God. They are incapable of loving God because they are spiritually dead.

The child of God is the only one who can love God with all of their heart because he is given the inner ability to do so. The Holy Spirit, who indwells the belief, provides the capability of loving God with all that we are. Loving God with all we are is evidence we belong to Him. It is a visible evidence that we belong to Him. This is what John meant when he said, **Anyone who loves is born of God and knows God. But anyone who does not love does not know. God——For God is love. (1 John 4:7-8)**

Chapter 14
The Glory of His Second Coming

We now come to the final chapter in our study of the glory of Christ. We now will look at the greatest event that will happen since the crucifixion and the resurrection of Jesus. It is the second coming of Jesus. There are many things that we can discuss concerning the future coming of Christ. We can talk about the various interpretations of his coming: whether he will come before the tribulation or during the middle of the tribulation. There are many books and resources we can use that espouse opinions of the second coming of Christ. For our purposes, I want us to look at what happens when He returns. We can debate all of the possibilities of events before His return. However, the only thing everyone agrees on concerning this event is IT WILL HAPPEN. Jesus is going to come back. It is the actual event of His coming I want us to look at,

Jesus promised that He would come again

As Jesus moved closer to His death on the cross, He spent time talking to his disciples about what was going to happen to him. He spent time telling them that he was going to be arrested by the religious leaders and that He was going to die. At the same time, he promised them that he was going to rise from the dead. It is obvious in reading the gospel accounts that the disciples did not understand when Jesus was talking about his death. They were disturbed about what would happen to them if he was not here with them. The more He talked about His death, the more concerned these disciples got. They had given up everything to follow Jesus. They left their boats, tax booths and other work to follow Him. Now, He is talking about dying. They suddenly realized that they were really going to be like sheep without a shepherd. Jesus then spends time comforting them with such a great promise. He is going to return and they were going to be with Him forever.

Jesus realizes that they are concerned about what they are hearing, so he gives them this wonderful promise. These disciples said, **Do not let your hearts be troubled. You believe in God, believe also in me. In my Father's house are many rooms. If it**

were not so, would I have told you that? Jesus is letting them know that He would not lie to them concerning heaven. He would not make something up just to make them feel better. He continues **and if I go and prepare a place for you, I will come again and will take you to myself, that where I am you may be also. (John 14:1-4. ESV)**

Notice in this passage that Jesus says believe in me. Believe that I will always be truthful and honest with you. Trust me to do what I say I will do. Trust me that my death will not be then end, but it is simply a door way to reach the glory of heaven. If then, we say that we believe in Jesus, then we also must believe that He is coming again. We don't know the time or the day, but we know the Who. We know Jesus, and we believe His word. He said He would be back. Therefore, those of us who are believers should pray like John in Revelation; even so, **Lord Jesus, come quickly.** This should be our desire. We want to see Him.

His coming will be visible to all

When the New Testament speaks about the coming of the Lord, it usually uses the word "Apocalypses." It is a word that means "Unveiling." The coming of Jesus unveils him so that He can be seen. His coming will not be some secret event that happens, and the world does not know about it. It is a public even where everyone will experience it in one way or another. The Christian will "be changed in a blink of the eye" and "will be caught up to meet the Lord in the air." Those who are not caught up will be left behind. The Christian will meet the Lord in the air as a moment of celebration and victory. Those left behind will meet the Lord not in celebration and victory but in fear and anxiety. They will not meet the Lord as a friend, but as someone who rebelled against Him by refusing the salvation, He offered.

For the Lord Himself will descend from heaven with a cry of command, with the voice of an archangel, and with the trumpet of God. And the dead in Christ will rise first. Then we who are alive, who are left will be caught up together with them in the clouds to meet the Lord in the air and so shall we ever

be with the Lord. Therefore, comfort one another with these words. (1 Thessalonians 4:16-18. ESV)

Behold, He is coming with clouds and every will we see Him, even those who pierced him, and all the tribes of earth will wail on account of Him, Even so Amen. (Revelation 1:7 ESV_

Many of the scriptures regarding the second coming refer to Jesus coming in the clouds. (Matthew 24:30, Matthew 26:64, Acts 1:9). The reference to the Lord's coming in the clouds speaks of majesty, glory, and power. God is often represented as appearing in the clouds.

Now Mount Sinai was wrapped in smoke because the Lord had descended on it in fire. The smoke of it went up like the smoke in a kiln and the whole mountain trembled greatly. (Exodus 19:18. ESV)

He made darkness his covering, his canopy around him, thick clouds dark with water. (Psalm 18:11)

With HIs coming, the inference is that as Jesus comes in the clouds, the world will be able to see Him. It is as though the clouds cover the earth and then Jesus steps through revealing His glory. **It is then that every eye will see Him, and every knee will bow down and confess that He is the Lord of Lords and King of Kings.**

Not only is there going to be the unveiling of the Lord Himself but there will be the revealing of all the blessings that God has waiting for us. Paul writes about this in his letter to the Philippians. **That in the ages to come, he might show the exceeding riches of His grace in his kindness toward us through Christ Jesus. (Philippians 2:7 KJV)**

The signs and warnings concerning His coming

Even though our Lord never told us the date of His coming, He did tell us that there will be signs and indicators which will alert us to His coming. In looking through the scripture some of these signs have been going on since Jesus ascended into heaven. Because it has been 2000 years since Jesus made the promises of His coming again, there have been doubters, naysayers and critics who argue that Jesus did not speak of a literal second coming. He was speaking allegorically. Others argue that His coming is fantasy and myth. Other critics state that these warnings Jesus gave about His return are things that have been happening since the start of civilization.

Jesus Made a list of the signs to look for.

The gospel will be preached around the world. There are not many places in our world that have not heard about the gospel. Yes, there are some, but most of the world has had a witness concerning the gospel of Jesus.

The persecution of believers. Once again, this has been happening since the establishment of the church. The persecution of believers is hard to read about or imagine. In Rome, Christians were used in gladiator games and targets for sport. In other arenas, Christians were gathered in the arena just before wild, hungry animals were turned loose on them. That was at the beginning of the history of the church. Since those early events, the world has become more radical in its hatred for Christianity. Christians are experiencing the worst kind of persecution by being burned alive in the Middle East, put in prison camps in North Korea, jailed for preaching the gospel in China, and beheaded by jihadist extremists. It is true these kinds of horrors have been going on since the founding of the church, but because of instant news and social media, we can see these events happening in real-time. These platforms seem to encourage Christian haters to be more bold in their actions against the children of God.

A falling away of believers. According to the New Testament, one of the saddest signs is that the church is going to lose its passion for the gospel and worship. Many will have little or no knowledge of the word of. God. Biblical illiteracy is growing at a catastrophic rate. We have now reached a time in our culture where many Christians cannot give an answer as to what they believe and why. Some know only the basics about Jesus: his birth, His death, His dying on the cross, His resurrection and His coming again. Beyond this basic information, many are not able to answer some of the deeper questions of their faith. It is the falling away that Paul is referring to.

When there is a neglect of the reading and the study of the Word of God, those who profess to be Christians will have no knowledge or any inspiration from the Word to help them in their journey away from the Lord. Some preachers and commentators believe that Paul is speaking about those who were never Christians to begin with. They state that a true belief will not depart from the truth. Yes, they will sin and fail at times in their life, but they still hold on to what they know about Jesus. They still have a desire to do better in their life.

When there is no adequate Bible knowledge then there is no way the believer can use the world to help him resist temptation or give a reasonable answer for his faith. This is why Paul said **they give heed to seducing spirits.** The seducing spirits mentioned here may refer to false teachings that would corrupt the Christian mind. These seducing spirits or teachers encourage believers to short-change their lives by seeking things that do not satisfy. C.S. Lewis compared indifferent believers as half-hearted creatures, fooling about with drink and sex and ambition when infinite joy is offered us, like an ignorant child who wants to go on making mud pies in a slum because he cannot imagine what is meant by the offer of a holiday at sea. We are far too easily pleased. (C/S. Lewis, The Weight of Glory and Other Addresses (Grand Rapids: Eerdmans, 1965)

This is a good illustration of those who claim to be believers but have a greater interest in entertainment, social standing, and money rather than giving effort and attention to knowing the Lord. This kind of behavior is an indication that the coming of the Lord is close. Any pastor who stands and preaches the gospel should passionately encourage believers not to settle for mud pies but for the glorious promises that come from the heart of God.

The reason Jesus is coming back

To gather his church. Jesus wants his people to be with Him. He wants us to experience the fullness of his presence and the utter joy of being in the presence of God. **And if I go and prepare a place for you, I will come again and will take you to myself, that where I am you may be also. (John 14:3 NIV).**

He is coming to judge those who refused Him as savior. It is sad to hear so many people say that it does not really matter what you believe as long as you are sincere in that belief. This idea is anathema to what Jesus said. In John 3:17, Jesus said, **For God did not send his son into the world to condemn the world, but that the world through Him would be saved. And he who believes in Him will not be condemned, but he who does not believe is condemned already BECAUSE HE HAS NOT BELIEVED IN THE ONLY BEGOTTEN SON OF GOD.** In spite of what some may say concerning how to be saved, Jesus said if a person does not believe in Him, he is commended already. It is not that he is going to be condemned. He is condemned already. What a terrible condition to be in: CONDEMNED. It does matter what you believe. It matters even more who you believe.

He's coming to separate the believers from the unbelievers, the saved from the unsaved and the condemned.

<u>31</u>When the Son of Man comes in His glory, and all the angels with Him, He will sit on His glorious throne. <u>32</u>All the nations will be gathered before Him, and He will separate the people one from another, as a shepherd separates the sheep from the goats. <u>33</u>He will place the sheep on His right and the goats on His left. Then the King will say to those on His right, 'Come, you who are blessed by My Father, inherit the kingdom prepared for you from the foundation of the world. <u>35</u>For I was hungry and you gave Me something to eat, I was thirsty and you gave Me something to drink, I was a stranger and you took Me in, <u>36</u>I was naked and you clothed Me, I was sick and you looked after Me, I was in prison and you visited Me.' Then the righteous will answer Him, 'Lord, when did we see You hungry and feed You, or thirsty and give You something to drink? <u>38</u>When did we see You a stranger and take You in, or naked and clothe You? <u>39</u>When did we see You sick or in prison and visit You?' And the King will reply, 'Truly I tell you, whatever you did for one of the least of these brothers of Mine, you did for Me.'

41Then He will say to those on His left, 'Depart from Me, you who are cursed, into the eternal fire prepared for the devil and his angels. **42**For I was hungry and you gave Me nothing to eat, I was thirsty and you gave Me nothing to drink, **43**I was a stranger and you did not take Me in, I was naked and you did not clothe Me, I was sick and in prison and you did not visit Me.'

44And they too will reply, 'Lord, when did we see You hungry or thirsty or a stranger or naked or sick or in prison, and did not minister to You?'

45Then the King will answer, 'Truly I tell you, whatever you did not do for one of the least of these, you did not do for Me.'

46And they will go away into eternal punishment, but the righteous into eternal life." (Matthew 25:31-46 KJV)

All of this scripture tells us of the return of our Lord. This should excite us to know that we will soon this this one whom we have never seen. Let us be ready. Let us anticipate His coming. As stated in an earlier chapter, we are filled with the glory of God because of the presence of the Holy Spirit living in us. However, when Jesus comes, we will experience the fullness of His glory because we will be completely transformed into His likeness.

As I write this, I think about that wonderful old song that says

What a day that will be,

When my Jesus I shall see,

And I look upon His face,

The One who saved me by His grace;

When He takes me by the hand,

And leads me through the Promised Land,

What a day, glorious day that will be.

There'll be no sorrow there,

No more burdens to bear,

No more sickness, no more pain,

No more parting over there;

But forever I will be,

With the One who died for me,

What a day, glorious day that will be.

What a day that will be,

When my Jesus I shall see,

When I look upon His face,

The One who saved me by His grace;

When He takes me by the hand,

And leads me through that Promised Land,

What a day, glorious day that will be

Oh What a day that will be,

When my Jesus I shall see,

When I look upon His face,

The One who saved me by His grace;

When He takes me by the hand,

And leads me through that Promised Land,

What a day, glorious day that will be. (What a day that will be; Lyrics and music written by Jim Hill, Ben Speer Music Company, 1955)

Closing Remarks

For God, who commanded the light to shine out of darkness, hath shined in our hearts, to *give* the light of the knowledge of the glory of God in the face of Jesus Christ. (2 Corinthians 4:6 KJV)

This verse gives the reason Paul preached and wrote the way he did.

He did it because of where he got his message. All that he knew came directly from God Himself. The doctrine and interpretation of scripture came from the light of God that invaded his life. The understanding of Gods working in the world did not come from human reasoning. It all came from God, who shined in his heart and illuminated the darkness of his mind. The light that was in Paul's life was the person of Jesus. Because the glory of Jesus lived in Paul's life, he felt compelled to tell the story of God's salvation for the world.

If men were left to themselves, they would continue to run headlong into sin and corruption. We would run deeper and deeper into the darkness of sin and shame. We would move away from God instead of toward Him. We need a change of direction in our lives. We need a different leadership instead of depending on our own moral compass. If we are going to live in freedom from sin and spiritual victory, we must follow the only one who can lead us there. The way we follow Jesus is to spend time reading and meditating on his word. We follow Him by spending time in prayer and communicating with Him. The more we practice these spiritual disciples, the more we're going to know Jesus in a deeper and more intimate way. The more we know Him and get close to Him, the more His glory is going to shine through us, revealing Him to the world around us.

This glory of Jesus reveals the wonder of worship. It reveals the beauty and power of the word of God. Men and women will sense the change in us because Jesus is revealing Himself through us. So may we be committed to getting as new to the Lord as we can, so others can see this glory that is in us.

Bibliography

Beacon Bible Commentary, Beacon Hill Press of Kansas City, Kansas. City Missouri, 1967

(Church Dogmatics: The Doctrine of the Word of God, Part 2. Karl Barth. Hendrickson Publishing, Marketing LLC. 2012)

John Gill Commentary on Colossians

Karl Barth, Church Dogmatics; Doctrine of Reconciliation Hendrickson Publishing, Marketing LLC, 2012

Barnes Notes on Galatians, Albert Barnes, Baker Publishing 1983)

When Hell Was In Session, Admiral Jeremiah Denton, WND Publishers, November 2009)

A chance to say goodby: Hope for grieving parents; written by Janice Kerlee, January 4, 2004)

The Great Awakening; 1725-1760, Phil Ryken, October 24, 1999)

(Lenski's New Testament Commentary—The interpretation of St Pauls Epistles to the Galatians, to the Ephesians and to the Philippians, Pg 262)

(C/S. Lewis, The Weight of Glory and Other Addresses (Grand Rapids: Eerdmans, 1965)

9 781965 560259